THE
SPANISH
TABLE

THE SPANISH TABLE

TRADITIONAL RECIPES AND WINE PAIRINGS FROM SPAIN AND PORTUGAL

STEVE WINSTON

GIBBS SMITH
TO ENRICH AND INSPIRE HUMANKIND
Salt Lake City | Charleston | Santa Fe | Santa Barbara

First Edition
1 2 3 4 5   09 10 11 12 13

Text © 2009 Steve Winston
Photo on page 89 © Horst Widlewski

Published by
Gibbs Smith
P.O. Box 667
Layton, Utah 84041

Orders: 1.800.835.4993
www.gibbs-smith.com

Designed by Debra McQuiston
Printed and bound in Hong Kong
Gibbs Smith books are printed on either recycled,
100% post-consumer waste, or FSC-certified papers

Library of Congress Cataloging-in-Publication Data

Winston, Steve.
The Spanish Table : traditional recipes and wine pairings from
Spain and Portugal / Steve Winston. — 1st ed.
p. cm.
ISBN-13: 978-1-4236-0373-3
ISBN-10: 1-4236-0373-7
1. Cookery, Spanish. 2. Cookery, Portuguese. 3. Wine and wine
making—Spain. 4. Wine and wine making—Portugal.
I. Spanish Table (Store) II. Title.
TX723.5.S7W57 2009
641'.5946—dc22
2008041293

My wife Sharon and I, as owners of The Spanish Table, would like to dedicate this cookbook, with a toast, to the extended family of The Spanish Table: employees, ex-employees, customers, and vendors with whom we have socialized during and after hours.

Good food and wine make good friends!

Contents

Introduction

The Spanish Table

We went to Iberia on a whim. Once we were there, we fell in love with the food and wine. That was in 1985, more than twenty years ago. We have been back at least once a year every year since. It immediately changed the way we cooked. After that first trip, the flavors we sought and the aromas we longed for were forever altered.

But we found that it was difficult after that first trip to find authentic ingredients to prepare dishes like those we remembered from our trip to Iberia or to find much variety of Spanish and Portuguese wines in the United States.

Sometimes an idea takes over your life. The idea for The Spanish Table was an idea like that. It started because we were frustrated buying ingredients for Spanish cooking. It became one of those litanies, "Someone should open a store to sell these things." In 1995, it evolved into, "We should open a store," when President Clinton offered federal employees early retirements.

So in September 1995, I retired from the United States Customs Service and opened the first The Spanish Table shop in Seattle. I was hoping that there were plenty of other people for whom the foods of Spain and Portugal were special enough to warrant them going out of their way to buy ingredients, utensils, and wines.

For the first two years, it seemed we were wrong. Business was slow and bills accumulated. Luckily, I had my federal pension to live on, but the

shelves of groceries imported from Spain were not exactly flying out the door. Then in January 1998, *Saveur Magazine* placed The Spanish Table on its first "Saveur 100" list. Our idea had been vindicated and The Spanish Table had been discovered. Business finally took off, and over the past several years we have opened three other shops: in Berkeley, Santa Fe, and Mill Valley, California.

Author's Note

As much as I love to read cookbooks, I am probably the worst sort of cook to write one. When I have something I want to cook, or want an idea for something to cook, I tend to consult a few cookbooks, perhaps take some cryptic notes on a scrap of paper, and start cooking.

This happens when I buy something at a farmers market or in an ethnic grocery store, or order something in a restaurant and decide it would be nice to cook something like that at home. Otherwise, I tend to just look around the kitchen for what is there and throw something together.

I have had no formal schooling in cooking. I tend not to measure things, to forget to set the timer when putting something in the oven, and to decide when to turn things over on the barbecue based on how much wine is left in the glass I poured for myself just after I put them on the grill.

When we opened The Spanish Table, people began to ask

me for advice. The first year we were open, one woman actually called me up as she was making her first paella and wanted me to stay on the line coaching her until it was finished. When we finally hung up, I decided it was time to write down my paella recipe.

That was the first of many recipes I was to write down for my customers. Gradually, I began to gain nerve enough to include them in our newsletters. At first they were the obvious recipes people asked for: Paella, Clams Cataplana, and Tortilla Española. Then the recipes began to get a little more creative based on those nights I would wander home with a bag of products sold by The Spanish Table or samples sent to us of products someone thought The Spanish Table should sell. I might, for example, find myself asking, "What can I do with a jar of cardoons? A jar of chestnuts?"

In order to write recipes, I had to discipline myself. I had to measure, time, remember, and take notes. Not an easy task for someone with my attention span. I even had to stop watching television while I was cooking.

At some point, we began to assemble some of the recipes into handouts we could give customers. Still, most of the recipes, once used in a newsletter, just languished on the hard drive of whatever computer was being used when it was written.

Cleaning up the hard drive on a computer we were discarding, I was surprised to find that over the past ten years I had written down more than a hundred different recipes. So we thought, why not compile them into a cookbook?

Let's cook!

¡Vamos a cocinar! Vamos cozinhar!

—*Buena suerte*

INGREDIENTS

The Spice Cabinet

Certain elements of aroma and flavor tend to distinguish Spanish and Portuguese cuisine from other similar cuisines. The following items contribute to that notable and tasty difference:

Saffron (*azafrán/açafrão*)

Saffron is the stigma plucked from the blossom of a fall blooming crocus that thrives in only a few micro-climates. There are three stigmas per purple crocus flower. In Spain, it is graded by quality and certified by a *Consejo Regulador*. Most grocery store saffron is Sierra or "B" grade. Ask for Mancha Grade saffron, unless you use saffron powder, which, because of its increased surface area, loses its flavor and aroma more rapidly and is vulnerable to adulteration. Saffron is almost impossible to measure and is added by the pinch.

Start with a pinch of 24–48 threads, or the stigmas of eight to sixteen blossoms. The grade of the saffron and its freshness will be a contributing factor. As with all spices, smell the saffron before using it and adjust accordingly. You will soon learn how much saffron you like—as it grows on you, it will probably be more not less.

Sweeteners

Single Flower Honey *(miel/mel)*

In Spain, bud-break begins very early in the south and proceeds northward until it reaches the highest elevations of the Pyrenees. Every year migratory beekeepers follow the blooms, placing their hives first in the eucalyptus groves of Huelva, later in the fragrant orange groves around Valencia, and then on the hills of Aragón where the wild rosemary

blooms as well as in the chestnut groves of Galicia. The honey is removed from the hives prior to each move. Each batch of honey is sampled by a taster and samples from the best lots are sent to be inspected under a microscope to be certified by the distinct shape of each flower's pollen. About 1 percent of the honey—the purest, most aromatic and distinctly flavored—is bottled as varietal, single-flower, gourmet honey. They are available from the blooms of lavender, rosemary, eucalyptus, thyme, chestnut, and, my favorite, orange blossom.

Membrillo
This is quince fruit jelly. Like the apple, which it resembles, the quince is naturally high in pectin. It is eaten like jam, but it is best known for being paired with manchego cheese.

Paellero
Saffron is included in paellero, a packaged paella seasoning mix marketed by every spice company in Spain. One envelope of paellero seasons four servings of paella. I have found that I can pretty much substitute paellero almost any time a recipe calls for saffron. Paellero is made up of garlic, salt, sweet paprika, corn flour, yellow food coloring, pepper, clove, and saffron.

Pebrella (*thymus piperella*)
This plant is a member of the thyme family that is indigenous to a narrow micro-climate stretching roughly from Valencia to Alicante. If you do not have pebrella, use thyme (*tomillo*) or oregano (*orégano/orégão*) or a combination of those two herbs.

Bay (*laurel/loureiro*)
European bay has a broader leaf and a smoother flavor than California bay. A bay leaf, or several, is a *muy típica* addition when cooking and basting.

Garlic (*ajo/alho*)
The Spanish use a purple-skinned garlic that is milder and sweeter than our common white-skinned garlic, which has a longer shelf life. Either garlic should be used liberally.

When a recipe calls for chopped raw garlic it is probably for the texture. Raw garlic is crunchy and pungent.

Many times, Spanish cooks brown garlic cloves—whole, slightly crushed, or sliced—in olive oil, then remove them before proceeding with the recipe. They may be added back later or just discarded. When using this technique, leave the pieces large so they can be easily removed with a slotted spoon.

When a recipe calls for minced garlic, feel free to use a garlic press. My wife does.

LA MANCHA SAFFRON

We went to visit our saffron supplier, Antonio Sotos, in Albacete one October when the saffron crocus were in bloom to see them harvested. Early our first morning there, just after the sun had risen, he drove us down a narrow farm road. As we rounded a bend, there, tucked in among the fields of corn, was a patch of fall-blooming saffron crocus. An old man was bent over the rows, a basket between his feet, plucking the small, purple blooms. Later that same morning, he would detach the three stamens from each flower and dry them the same day. If each step is perfect, if there is no rain, if the stamens don't break, his saffron will end up in Antonio's vault where the dried stamens are stored until they are sold. The pungent scent of the saffron was so strong that it burned our eyes, making them water, when we stepped inside.

Parsley (*perejil/salsa*)

A tablespoon of minced parsley, because it contains chlorophyll, is often the secret ingredient that gives a dish a fresh taste. I prefer to use flat-leaf parsley rather than the crinkly leafed version, but the important thing is to add a little to dishes wherever, and whenever, possible.

For the Moorish touch, substitute mint (*hierba buena*) for some or all of the parsley in recipes.

Cilantro (*cilantro/coentros*)

Cilantro is used extensively in the cuisine of the Canary Islands and Portugal but seldom on the Spanish mainland. It is used like parsley.

Cumin (*comino/cominhos*)

One of the "Moorish" spices, cumin pops up as a seasoning in dishes in the regions the Moors occupied some 500 years ago and long after they retreated from Granada.

Rosemary (*romero/rosmainho*)

Rosemary grows wild in the hills of Spain, flavors the honey of bees, the flesh of lambs, and is used here and there in Spanish cooking.

Farcellets

The Catalan version of *bouquet garni*, a farcellet is a collection of local aromatic herbs, twigs, and sprigs of savory, thyme, and wild oregano wrapped in laurel leaves and tied with string. These make an amazing difference when added to the stock pot, imparting a full range of subtle herbal flavors.

Salt and Pepper
Sea Salt (*sal/sal*)

Both the Portuguese and the Spanish tend to use salt and olive oil liberally. When people come in to the store and say they are having trouble recreating a dish they had on their travels, I tell them to try adding a little more salt and a little more olive oil. Sea salt crystals come in a variety of sizes.

Black Pepper (*pimento/preta*)

You do not find Spanish cooks using much black pepper. This is a quirk rendered even quirkier by the fact that Columbus set sail in search of a sea route to the East Indies to obtain black pepper and other spices. Since we live in the United States where waiters circle restaurants with foot-long pepper grinders under their arms searching for a yet un-peppered dish, I have used it occasionally in recipes for this book.

Condiments
Capers (*alcaparras/alcaparras*)

The caper is the flower bud of a low-growing, woody bush picked before they flower. They basically cost "per each." That is, the smaller the caper, the more expensive the jar. The smallest have the most intense flavor. The largest have the softest texture. They are packed in either brine or salt. Rinse the brine-packed capers before using. Soak the salt-packed capers in water for 15 minutes, and then rinse them before using.

Caperberries

The caperberry is the fruit of the caper bush, appearing after they have flowered. The berries are frequently served just as they are as a tapa in bars in southern Spain, consumed like olives. They can also be sliced or chopped and used in cooking and salads.

The Pantry

Nuts

Marcona almonds (*alemndras/amêndoas*)

Unique to Spain, Marcona almonds are broader and flatter than the more common commercially sold almonds, and they have a hard protective shell that resists insects so well that they may be grown naturally without herbicides.

Hazelnuts (*avellanas/avelãs*)

Black-skinned *negreta* hazelnuts are grown in Catalonia, particularly around Tarragona. They have a rich flavor.

Pine Nuts (*piñones/pinhões*)

European pine nuts are creamy colored from top to bottom and have a rich flavor. Toasted and sprinkled over everything from salad to white beans, they make a simple dish more elegant.

Chufa

Chufas, also known as tiger nuts, are a nut-size tuber grown around Valencia and in North Africa. Valencians grind them to make horchata, a refreshing summer beverage the color of milk but quite dissimilar in taste. They also freeze horchata for ice cream. They swear by its healthy properties because horchata de chufa is high in fiber, protein, minerals, and vitamins E and C.

Chestnuts (*castañas/castanhas*)

The sprawling limbs of chestnut trees dominate many a Spanish landscape. The nuts are harvested in the fall and roasted on the streets and sold for snacks, but they make a welcome addition to many soups and stews as well.

Rice
Valencian Rice
This Mediterranean rice is similar to Italy's Aborio rice. Medium- to short-grained, it can be boiled in an open, uncovered pot, either a paella pan or a cazuela. While Italian cooks and chefs prefer to stir the pot for risotto, the Spanish leave well enough alone, letting the rice crust on either the bottom, if cooked on top of the stove, or the top, if cooked in an oven *al horno.* Buy Valencian rice labeled "extra." It is the highest grade, without broken grains, and it cooks evenly.

Bomba Rice
Bomba is the parent of the two hybrids that are marketed as Valencian rice. It is hard to grow because it is low yield and is not disease resistant, so it is grown by small farmers in isolated plots and is usually hand harvested.

Bomba had been almost extinct as a crop when it was rediscovered by the chefs of fancy restaurants in Barcelona, where cost is not a fatal barrier. Bomba absorbs three to four parts water to one part rice, one and a half or so times what the hybrid rices absorb. This means a more intensely flavored rice dish when it is cooked in stock as in paella. I have come to only use bomba for paella-style cooking.

Brown Rice
Occasionally brown rice from Spain is sold in the United States. It is delicious, nutty flavored, and firm textured, but it takes twice as long to cook, so allow 50 minutes for cooking time if using it in one of our recipes.

Stale Bread
Yesterday's *pan duro*, *pão seco*, is essential to Spanish and Portuguese cuisine. A tip: slice or cube the bread before it is really stale and it will not disintegrate into crumbs. Dry bread stores well and can be frozen.

Legumes
Beans, Garbanzos, and Lentils
The Spanish treat beans as gourmet food. If using dry beans, soak to plump them before cooking. The longer it has been since they were harvested, the longer they should soak. Drain, rinse, and then cover them with water plus an additional inch, and cook slowly. Jarred cooked beans from Spain are of very high quality and an easy kitchen shortcut. Their flavor will be even better if you stir in a little Spanish extra virgin olive oil just before serving.

Pocha Beans
Pochas are round shell beans that are harvested just as they reach maturity. They are then cooked and canned without being dried. Good quality pochas are creamy white with a residual green blush from the chlorophyll still remaining from when they were picked, thus the source of their name, which means "faded" in Spanish.

Pardina Lentil (*lenteja*)
The name refers to the flat, dull, duff color of the lentil, or, *pardo*, in Spanish. They are available as an import or from specialty legume growers in the United States. European lentils are smaller than the larger North American variety and retain their shape when cooked, making them easy to use in salads and as side dishes.

Tolosana Beans
The village of Tolosa in the Basque Country is the origin of these red *riñonada* beans, which are now grown even in Idaho.

Garrafón, Granja, Judión, Fava Beans
Big broad white beans are known by a variety of names across Spain. They may be distinct clones or not; only the seed vendor knows. They are buttery and expand to magnificent size as they soak. The Spanish will apparently pay anything for the best specimens of

these beans, which often sell, on a per-serving cost, for much more than saffron.

Old-World Beans

Garbanzo Beans

The garbanzo is an old-world bean, predating Columbus' return from the New World. Recipes using garbanzos often can be traced back to the Moors.

Habitas

The fava bean is another old-world bean. Picked early in the spring, baby favas, or *habitas*, are a Spanish delicacy that are cooked and canned. Picked at maturity and dried, they are available both with and without their naturally tough skins.

Lupini Bean (*altramuz, tremoco*)

Sold as snacks on the streets of Portugal and Spain, you pop the bean out of its skin and into your mouth as Mediterraneans have been doing for 2,000 years.

Some Unusual Canned Vegetables

Green Garlic Shoots (*brotes*)

You are starting to see green garlic shoots in farmer's markets in the United States come early spring. They are a true delicacy having a subtle green vegetable flavor suffused with mild garlic. They are canned and sold in jars in Spain, which is not only handy but extends its availability beyond spring. Garlic shoots make tasty tapas when combined with prawns and eggs or with mushrooms and eggs. Just sauté, scramble, and season to taste.

Borage Stems (*borraja*)

Borage stems are a little exotic to Americans, but they are part of the ancient Spanish heritage of foraging for greens. For simplicity, heat the borage stems in their juice, drain, and add olive oil. They are also quite good when cooked with potatoes or combined with scrambled eggs.

Cardos /Cardoons /Thistles

Cardos are popular in Navarra, where they are associated with Christmas Eve dinner, probably because the harvest starts in November and extends through the winter.

Like their relative the artichoke, the *cardo* is a member of the thistle family. Cardoons even provide vegetable rennet used to make some Spanish cheeses like *Torta del Casar.*

White Asparagus (*espárragos blanco/ espargo branco*)

Grown without exposure to light, asparagus spears remain white, their chlorophyll undeveloped. This was once accomplished by mounding dirt over the emerging stalks, but now black plastic is used. The pale spears are a luxury used mostly in salads but also in simple fish dishes. Spears are sold by size, and containers usually indicate how many they contain. The fewer in a container, the larger and more expensive they are.

Peppers

Piquillo Peppers

Piquillo means pointed. The piquillo pepper originated on the farms surrounding the Navarran village of Lodosa on the north bank of the Ebro River east of Logroño. It was a pepper grown to be roasted and preserved. Its piquant flavor is unique and quintessentially Spanish. Its firm flesh and narrow shape lends itself to stuffing.

To stuff piquillos, hold the empty pepper vertically in the circle formed by the thumb and index finger and use a demitasse spoon to ease the mixture inside. Once mastered, this process only takes a moment.

Morrón Peppers

The morrón is a thick-fleshed sweet pepper that is roasted. Use them as you would a roasted red bell pepper or where recipes call for pimento.

Padrón Peppers

Originating in the Galician fishing village of Padrón, these fresh green peppers are picked while young and still small. They are then fried in olive oil, salted, and served by the dozen as a tapa. If properly grown, the peppers are generally mild, but in each dozen there lurks a hot one. One of the amusements of a Spanish tapa bar is watching others to see who will bite into a hot pepper. There are now several farmers growing padrón peppers in the United States.

Ñora Peppers

The ñora is a round, red, sweet cherry pepper that, after being dried, is ground into sweet pimentón. It is most often grown in the Catalonia, Valencia, and Alicante regions. A ñora, stemmed and seeded, is often tossed in the pot when making stocks, soups, and stews, and then discarded much as one would, in France, use and discard a *bouquet garni*. The flavor it leaves behind is elusive but sweet, rich, and lingering.

Choricero Peppers

Also known as *cristal* peppers, these are picked when red and then dried in *ristras* hung from the eves of homes in the north of Spain and the Basque Country. These look exactly like the New Mexican pepper ristras seen every fall when we visit our store in Santa Fe. However, the Spanish pepper is mild, much milder, than the New Mexican pepper. Choricero peppers are available dry and as a thick paste sold in jars. The paste lends a rich, deep subtext, often unidentifiable, when added to dishes in small quantities.

Guindilla Peppers

This term encompasses several long, narrow peppers including the tiny bird's eye–shaped *cayena* pepper used to add heat to *gambas al ajillo*, and the long (5–6 inches) hot pepper ground for *pimentón picante*. What guindillas have in common is that, to the Spanish palate at least, they are spicy.

Pimentón

Spanish paprika, *pimentón*, comes in three types: sweet (*dulce*), bittersweet (*agridulce*) and hot (*picante*) ground to a powder from three types of red peppers. It adds depth to sauces and stews, enriching meats from sausage to grilled chicken, and adding bright color to paella and salads.

Basque Green Guindilla del Norte Peppers

The Basques place a small bowl of these peppers on the table as a condiment for beans and other dishes. The diner chops them up himself and sprinkles the pieces over the dish in quantities to his own taste. They are similar to Italy's pepperoncini peppers.

PIRI PIRI PEPPER SAUCE

In Portugal there are restaurants that serve nothing but grilled chicken basted with piri piri pepper sauce. The chicken usually comes with a side of home fries. If the roasted chicken isn't hot enough, there are bottles of piri piri sauce on the table to further ignite your taste buds. If things get too hot, it is okay because one can always order a tall Sagres beer to wash it all down. These very informal restaurants are delicious, cheap, and fun.

Piments De Pays

These skinny, green, "country" peppers are eaten fresh and cooked, in season, throughout the Basque Country in Spain and France.

Piment D'Espelette

This paprika pepper is grown in the Basque village of Esplette in Labourd, France.

Portuguese Peppers
Piri Piri

On their sailing ships, the Portuguese carried peppers from the New World to their colonies in Asia, Goa, and Macau, and on to Africa. In Angola and Mozambique, one little hot pepper was named pepper-pepper or "piri piri" in Swahili. From Africa it traveled to Portugal, where is it is used to season prawns and chicken.

Azorean Hot Finger Peppers

These long, slender, finger-length peppers come in both red and yellow. In the United States they are found packed whole in jars. A fairly thin and very salty crushed red pepper sauce, *Pimenta Moída*, is made from these finger peppers.

Olives
Table Olives

Olives that are generally used for eating include Arbequina, Empeltre, Cuquillo, Arágon, Morado, and, of course, Manzanilla. Some kinds of Portuguese table olives are Galega, Cordovil, Verdeal, Madural, and Cobrancosa.

Stuffed Olives

The Spanish are masters of the stuffed olives. Our top three favorites are, in order, piquillo pepper-stuffed, lemon-stuffed, and anchovy-stuffed. The piquillo-stuffed olives are a revelation in just how much flavor the pepper can contribute. The lemon-stuffed olives are great in salads and martinis and the anchovy-stuffed olives are a natural in Caesar and other salads. Also look for almond-stuffed olives as well as the ever increasing variety of flavors from garlic to salmon.

Olive Oil (*Aceite de Oliva*)

There are many kinds of olives (*aceitunas*) used to make olive oil. The olive harvest in any one area extends over several weeks, even months, so they are picked at varying degrees of ripeness. Two factors tend to influence the color of the oil (which ranges from grass greens to golden wheat in color):

OLIVE OIL

Modern technology has increased the percentage of olive oil that can be classified as extra virgin olive oil. Consequently there is not as much price difference between a gallon of extra virgin olive oil and a gallon of olive oil (the term pure, while still in common use, has been discarded by the olive oil industry). Pomace olive oil, on the other hand, is made by heating the pits and waste after "cold pressing" olive oil. It is cheap and tastes cheap.

the type of olive and the ripeness of the olive when it is picked. Olive oil is rated using a small, navy blue goblet with a glass cover. The goblet is cradled in the hands to warm it, the cover is removed, and the aroma is inhaled. The oil is then sipped. Notes are taken regarding its component attributes. Only then is the color noted.

The lower the acidity, the fruitier and richer the olive oil. By definition, extra virgin olive oil must have less than 1 degree of acidity, but premium, first-pressed olive oils have even less. Because of modern handling techniques and machinery, most olive oil pressed today qualifies as extra virgin olive

OLIVE TREES

Olive trees are everywhere in Spain, but it is in the south, from Jaén to Córdoba to Grenada, that, like armies in ranks, the olive trees march across Andalucía in enfilades. They stretch on and on over hill and dale, seemingly forever, disappearing off into the distance. As they reach the far horizon, the individual dots of their silhouettes blur together to form drab green stripes, each separated by a ribbon of blood-red earth.

Three thousand years ago the domesticated olive arrived as cuttings with the Phoenicians. They were planted around the ports and then spread from the coast, planted progressively farther north until they reached the Pyrenees. By Roman times, Andalucía had become an exporter of olive oil to the world and has remained so ever since.

oil. Olive oil is rich in vitamins A, E, D, and K. Some of the kinds of Spanish olives that are used for oil are Arbequina, Picada, Picual, Hojiblanca, Empeltre, Cornicabra, Manzanilla, Villalongo (Valencian Manzanilla), Necadillo Blanco, Blanqueta, and Sollana.

Choosing Olive Oil for Cooking

When cooking with olive oil, particularly when frying, remember that it expands when heated. Leave room. In this book I have used the following three clues as to the minimum quality olive oil to be used in a recipe.

Olive Oil for Frying

You can use the least expensive, quality olive oil available as the extended exposure to heat of frying drives off many of the olive flavors. However, food fried in olive oil is distinguishable in flavor from food fried in other oils. If embarking on a large frying project, there are blended oils, such as olive-canola, which can save you money.

Olive Oil

When olive oil is specified in a recipe, use a quality oil. It does not have to be extra virgin olive oil, but I usually use a less expensive brand of extra virgin olive oil because I think it gives dishes a better flavor.

Extra Virgin Olive Oil

Where extra virgin olive oil is specified in a recipe and is not going to be heated, use one of your best extra virgin olive oils. I keep three types on hand, ranging from buttery to pungent to use for various effects when finishing hot dishes or dressing salads as well as for dipping.

Vinegars

Spain and Portugal are wine countries, and wine vinegars predominate. Although in the north, where *sidra*, apple cider, both alcoholic and nonalcoholic, is fashionable, there is apple cider vinegar. Salad dressing is simply vinegar and oil in Spain, though commerce being what it is, I now see some of our Spanish purveyors offering premixed, bottle salad dressings similar to those you find in the United States.

Sherry

Sherry vinegar comes in a hierarchy of aging based on the solera system. *Lagrimas*, or tears, indicate that the origin of the grape juice is free-run (the juice that "weeps" from the grapes before they are crushed.) As with wines, what you put in directly affects what comes out.

Montilla

Like Montilla wines, the vinegars of Montilla are close cousins of sherry. Montilla PX wine, with its heady sweetness, produces a vinegar with concentrated brown sugar notes that is wonderful splashed on fresh fruit.

Wine

Spanish wine vinegars can be either white or red, and the red can be *crianza*, or barrel aged. Varietal red wine vinegars are also made from Garnacha or Cabernet grapes.

Rioja "Balsamic Process"

With the worldwide popularity of balsamic vinegars from Italy, the Spanish have adapted those techniques to vinegar production, particularly in Rioja.

Cava

The Catalans make great white vinegars from cava.

Muscat

The muscat grape produces a sweet wine that in turn produces a sweet vinegar with subtle depths of flavor.

Vermouth

Spain has had a long tradition of vermouth production, and recently some has found its way into the market as a vinegar. The herbal notes make it fun to use.

Odds and Ends
Apple Cider (*sidra/cidra*)

Along the north coast apple cider has a cult following with *siderias* specializing in pouring—from great height—glasses of hard cider that is fermented dry and left unfiltered so that is slightly cloudy. In Asturias, *sidra* also plays an important part in the cuisine.

Chicken Stock (*caldo*)

Spanish chicken stock, *caldo*, even the commercial versions, contain a bit of *jamón*, ham, for flavor, usually from throwing a chunk of bone into the stock pot (jamón bones are sawed into sections and sold by Spanish butchers just for such purposes). In fact, caldo was likely to be pretty much whatever was handy to be thrown into the pot. I have also been assured that chicken feet are not an option but, rather, a necessary addition. In any case, when making chicken stock, be sure to put a farcellet in the pot or include a sprig of thyme, a bay leaf or two, and a branch of parsley.

Fish Stock (*fumet*)

Fish stock can be prepared from bones and other trimmings of white fish, shrimp shells, or shellfish. This stock should be used immediately or frozen. A quick alternative is canned clam juice.

Smokehouse-Cured Meats
Jamón or jamón serrano

Serrano means *of the sierra*, or ham from the mountain, which is where it is cool and breezy enough to air cure a ham without it spoiling (salt also plays an early role in the curing of pig meat). Serrano hams hang for 12–18 months before they are sold.

JAMÓN

In a great many Spanish homes, a jamón is kept on the sideboard with a cloth draped over it between meals. Sitting like this, the surface dries out. When this happens, a thin slice is carved off and set to the side. Next the carver whittles away any excess fat and places that to the side. In a waste-not-want-not society, these parings are raw material for the cook. When at times it seems that a bit of ham goes into everything in Spain from soup to vegetables, it is probably because of the presence of these parings.

Jamón Iberico Bellota

Iberico is jamón made from the meat of the Spanish black-footed pig. Bellota indicates that the pig ate acorns. Jamón Iberico Bellota is very, very expensive, but it melts in your mouth like butter.

Lomo

Lomo is cured pork tenderloin. Although it looks like a sausage, it is a solid piece of lean and delicious meat.

Embutidos (sausages)
Chorizo

Spanish-style chorizo is lean with chunks of meat, and the flavor is dominated by pimentón and garlic. Mexican chorizo is not really a substitute, and Italian sausage is definitely not. There are two basic types of cures for Spanish chorizo: soft for cooking, and hard for slicing and eating without further preparation. A related sausage is cantimpalo—cantimpalito in its bite-size form.

Sobrasada

Sobrasada is a very soft, finely ground chorizo with a higher fat content and is intended to be spreadable. It makes great *montaditos*. Spread a little on a slice of bread and run it under the broiler.

Manteca Colorada

The fat content of manteca is close to pure lard. Flecked with bits of pork and colored by pimentón, it is spread on toast for breakfast. If it were available in the United States, it would be seized by the American Heart Association. It is that good.

Morcilla

A popular saying is that the Spanish villagers used everything but the squeal of the pig. This is more than a phrase since the pig protests his butchering by squealing. Following his vain protest, when only his squeal escapes, he is reduced with knives to meat. His blood is captured in a basin and is combined with either rice or onions and is formed into morcilla—blood sausage. When cured, morcilla turns black. You either like it or you don't.

Butifarra

Butifarra is white sausage from Catalonia made without pimentón. Every Catalan has a story about an uncle who made butifarra from pigs kept in the hills and fattened on the pomace, or waste, left after cold pressing olive oil. "They melted in your mouth," they would tell you.

Portuguese Sausages
Linguiça

Portugal's signature sausage is usually very lean with subtle seasonings.

Chouriço

The Portuguese version of chorizo. The Portuguese believe that adding slices of linguiça or chouriço will benefit any dish from clams to pot roast. Believe them.

Cheese
Spanish Cheeses (*queso*)

Most of the terrain in Spain is unfavorable to cows, so sheep dominate, followed by their scrambling compatriots, the goats. Therefore, many of the great cheeses of Spain are made from sheep's milk. Like bread, which starts as flour and water and ends up taking on so many forms, or wine, which starts as mere grape juice, cheese starts simply and diverges into myriad variations. There are more than eighty recognized Spanish cheeses.

Manchego

Manchego dominates the Spanish cheese industry. It is made from *manchega* sheep that are grazed on the high plains of La Mancha. The cheese is smooth and rich in oils. Mild when young, it becomes sharper and drier with age. The cross-hatched design on the waxed rind is intended to recall the esperato grass baskets in which it was once formed into wheels.

Other Sheep Cheeses
There are many other sheep cheeses from regions outside La Mancha, including Ibérico, Zamorano, and Tronchón. In the Basque Country, the *latxa* sheep are used to make Idiazabal.

Goat Cheeses
Spanish goat cheeses are a small production and very individual. The most widely distributed are the wine- or paprika-cured goat cheeses from Mucia, but also look for Garrotxa, Ibores, and Caña de Cabra.

Cow's Milk Cheeses
These cheeses originate from the rich valleys that provide pasture for cows in the Pais Vasco, Asturias, Galicia, and Catalonia. Look for Majón from the Balearic Islands, Úrgelia, Sán Simón, and Tetilla, which is formed in the shape of a woman's breast, much to the painter Juan Miró's reported delight.

Blue Cheeses
Cabrales and Valdeón are named for their respective villages in the *Picos de Europa*.

Portuguese Cheeses (*oueijo*)
Sheep cheeses dominate on the mainland of Portugal but cow's milk dominates in the Azores. São Jorge is the best known of the Azorean cheeses. Sêrra da Estrêla, Serpa, and Evora are excellent sheep cheeses. But my favorite Portuguese cheese is Palhais—small cheeses made from goat's milk.

Fish in Tins
Bonito Tuna (*atun/atum*)
Food writers are constantly discovering North Atlantic Bonito tuna canned in olive oil. It breathes new life into everything from a salad to a sandwich to old standards like tuna and rice or tuna noodle casserole.

Anchovies (*anchoas/anchovas*)
In grocery stores in Spain, canned anchovies are kept in the refrigerator. You should keep yours cool as they are considered *"semi curado."*

Mackerel (*caballas/carapau*)
The mackerel is another small fish high in those oils said to be good for your health.

Sardines (*sardinas/sardinhas*)
It is the packing in olive oil that distinguishes the Iberian sardine from all others.

Cod/Salt Cod (*bacalao/bacalhau*)
The Basques and Portuguese sailed to Newfoundland to catch cod, which was salted to preserve it. The resulting textural change has made salt cod a staple throughout the Hispanic world long after freezing fish became the norm.

Mussels (*mejillones/mexilões*)
Small mussels packed in vinegar, *escabeche*, are a mainstay of the tapa bar. The escabeche can be either mild or spicy.

Scallops (*vieiras/ vieiras*)
Saint James, *Santiago*, is represented by the scallop shell and the scallop is considered the official food of Santiago. It is often served as coquilles St. Jacques.

Cockles (*berberechos/berbigão*)
These are the babiest of baby clams, usually packed in brine.

Octopus (*pulpo/polvo*)
Chunks packed in olive oil only need a toothpick to be a tapa, though a dusting of pimentón will enhance them. Pulpo is traditionally served on a round wooden platter.

Squid (*calamare en su tinta/lula*)

Chunks of squid are packed with ample ink for making black rice and other dishes.

Angulas

These were once baby eels, but more likely today are surimi replicas that are spaghetti thin and pale white. In tapa bars they are served sizzling hot in olive oil with garlic and a little red guindilla pepper.

Boquerones

These white anchovy fillets are packed in vinaigrette. They require refrigeration.

Clam Juice

It is sold in bottles and small tins in most grocery stores. Because making Spanish dishes like paella can use a lot of clam juice, we stock large 46-ounce tins, which you may be able to find in stores catering to restaurants.

Snail (*caracoles/caracóis*)

The Spanish eat several types of sea snails, usually as tapas, by picking the flesh from the shell with a pin. However, it is land snails that show up often in paella. If you do not have a supply of snails living in your garden, Spanish snails are available in jars.

TOOLS

The Paella Pan

Until a generation ago, paella pans were still being made by hammering a round piece of metal over a wood form and rolling the edges by hand. The dimples in the bottom of modern machine-made paella pans are vestiges of the marks left by the hammer when shaping the metal.

Originally paella was a dish made in Valencia using chicken, rabbit, snails, and three kinds of fresh beans. It was a dish of the poor, of the cocina pobre: rice, wild rabbits from the snare, a netted bird, snails gathered from the dewy morning grasses, some chicken, or some other feathered friend. So at its origin, paella was merely rice flavored with foraged foods and leftovers. Gradually paella has come to be, in most people's mind, paella mixta, combining shellfish with chicken, sausage, and vegetables.

There are many, many paella recipes. There is no right or wrong recipe, only the recipe that pleases you. Even in Spain, paella ingredients vary from place to place and time to time, depending on local traditions and the ingredients available. Anything from fresh garden produce to holiday leftovers can inspire a cook to create an original version of this one-dish feast. You should use your imagination and the ingredients you have on hand and experiment.

Recipes for the Paella Pan

The Spanish Table's Classic Paella

5 threads saffron

1/2 cup warm dry white wine

2 tablespoons olive oil per serving capacity of the pan, enough to completely cover bottom of the pan when it is cool (the oil will expand as it heats)

1 piece chicken, such as a thigh

1 clove garlic, finely chopped

1/4 cup chopped onion

1/2 to 1 soft Spanish-style cooking chorizo

1/2 cup uncooked Valencian rice

1/2 teaspoon sweet or bittersweet pimentón

1/8 cup grated tomato (cut in half, grate, and discard the skin)

1 cup liquid per 1/2 cup rice, such as clam juice or water

1 cup chicken stock per 1/2 cup of rice, more if using bomba

2 shrimp and/or prawns

2 to 4 small clams and/or mussels

Cooked garrofón beans from Valencia (alubias), optional

Some vegetables: red piquillo or morrón peppers cut in strips, peas, green beans, and/or artichoke hearts

Minced parsley for garnish

Lemon wedges for garnish

This style of paella is what most people associate with the name. Paella is cooked in a pan by adding ingredients progressively and allowing their flavors to merge and mingle and be absorbed into the rice. Ingredients are never removed once they are added. Exception: when using a pan slightly beyond its capacity, I remove the chicken pieces and keep them warm until everything else is in the pan and then I put them back on top where they can float on the surface, rising slightly above the rim of the pan. ☺ Measurements are per serving so use this list as a multiplication table.

1 Dissolve the saffron in the wine and set aside.

2 At a medium temperature, heat the olive oil in a paella pan that is large enough to hold the number of servings you need. Add chicken and fry, turning, until golden brown. When chicken juice runs clear, add garlic and onions and sauté until translucent. Add chorizo and cook until heated through and beginning to sweat fat. Then add the rice and pimentón, stirring until well coated with oil, about one minute. Add the grated tomato followed by the liquid, stock, and the saffron and wine mixture. Bring to a boil, scraping the bottom of pan, and adjust heat to maintain a simmer. Add the seafood–pushing the clams hinge side down into the paella–then add beans and other vegetables you are using.

3 When you add the liquid, time for 25 minutes and then check to see if the rice is done. At this point, it is traditional to let the paella *dormir*, or rest, for 15 minutes while the cook has an aperitif. The paella is loosely covered, in Spain often with a section of the daily newspaper (but not the section with the soccer scores). I set a sheet of aluminum foil over the paella without crimping the edges so it can breathe a little.

4 Sprinkle with minced parsley, garnish with lemon wedges, and serve.

The Very Large Paella

Please refer to the facing page for specific ingredients and instructions for preparing the paella.

It is not hard to cook paella for a large group of people (I have made it for as many as forty before), once you steel your nerve and jump in. It may even be easier. Calculate the volume of your pan and decide how much cooked rice it can hold by measuring how much liquid it holds and then dividing by two. That will determine how much uncooked rice you can use. It is best to subtract 10 percent from this figure to provide room for the other ingredients you will be adding. Make a list of the ingredients you are using in the order you will add them to the pan. I keep everything in a big cooler by my feet until I use it and tape the checklist of ingredients to the top of it. Make sure you will have enough heat from whatever source you are using and that the pan will remain stable when filled. Then it is show time. Gather everyone around and start cooking.

If you think your heat source is marginal for the size pan you are using, bring the liquid to a boil before adding it. Otherwise, it is easier just to buy large containers of clam juice and/or chicken stock and pour them directly into the pan. Once, in a friend's backyard, I just used water and added it by filling the pan up using a garden hose. It added a charming element of flippancy.

Tip: When shopping for ingredients for a large paella, you can cut your prep time by the way you select them. I use chicken strips, which cook quickly and easily. Bags of individually frozen peas and beans can just be dumped in right from the bag. There are also bags of mixed seafood available in the frozen food section of the grocery store that contain shrimp, squid, mussels, and other seafood. They can be easily added to the pan once the liquid is boiling, even if they are still frozen. I dump in jars of things such as artichoke hearts, liquid and all. If adding a lot of liquid this way, you need to account for it in your "total liquid" computation.

Pebrella and Asparagus Paella with Shrimp and Prawns

SERVES 4

6 cups clam juice
1 tablespoon pebrella
1 head garlic, half the cloves crushed, skin left on, and half the cloves peeled and chopped
1 pound asparagus spears
1/2 pound large Mexican white prawns
1/2 cup Spanish olive oil
1/2 pound Alaska rock shrimp
1/2 pound Oregon shrimp meat
2 cups bomba rice

Pebrella is one of the native thymes unique to Spain.

1 Heat the clam juice with the pebrella and the crushed garlic in a stockpot. Break off the tough ends of the asparagus spears and toss the ends in the pot. Peel the prawns and toss the shells in the pot. Let this broth brew over a moderate heat while you heat the olive oil in a 13-inch or larger paella pan.

2 When oil is hot, add the chopped garlic and cook until golden brown. Add prawns and toss in the oil.

When prawns turn pink, add the asparagus, broken into one-inch sections, and toss. Add the shrimp and then stir in the rice.

3 Strain the broth, discarding the asparagus stalk butts, prawn shells, and pebrella leaves and ladle or pour it into the paella pan. Bring to a boil, reduce heat and simmer 20 minutes or until rice is done. Allow the paella ten minutes to *dormir* before serving.

Nieves' Paella

During one of our visits to Valencia, Nieves, the mother of our foreign-exchange student Xavi, decided to teach me how to make a proper *paella valenciana*. When I arrived at the family's flat at the appointed hour, she cleared her kitchen of bystanders and gave me a ruffled apron to wear. Nieves is a modern Spanish woman. She has a career, stylish clothes, and a sexy haircut, but in the kitchen she is as severely traditional as her mother or any of her aunts. At every step in the making of the paella, I was instructed in the correct way to proceed and the correct ingredients to use. She apologized because the snails, *caracoles*, were not gathered by her uncle; she had to substitute caracoles she purchased from a gypsy selling them in el mercado. They are a compromise. But most ingredients are correct and "of this place only." She was very firm on this point. A proper *paella* can only be made in Valencia. Even the water is different elsewhere.

Wild Mushroom Paella

SERVES 6 AS A SIDE DISH

¹/₂ cup olive oil
1 pound mushrooms, chanterelles
   or another flavorful wild variety,
   sliced
2 cups brown calasparra rice
¹/₂ cup Madeira wine
4 cups chicken stock
1 cup Picada (page 108)

This makes a great side dish in mushroom season. To elevate it to an entrée, add a pork tenderloin cut into cubes and browned in the oil before adding the mushrooms.

1 Heat olive oil in a 13-inch or larger paella pan. Add mushrooms, cook until limp, and then stir in the rice. Add Madeira and stock, and mix in picada. Bring to a boil, reduce heat, and cook at a brisk simmer for 50 minutes.

Fallas

The annual fiesta in Valencia is *Fallas*, a weeklong parade of papier-mâché floats that are ultimately burned. Our Santa Fe store manager participated in Fallas as a college project. This is her memory of the culmination of the fiesta:

"We walked around all the barrios to see the Fallas on their final night. As part of tradition we were not allowed to sleep because we were participants in the *fallero*. The firemen hosed down all the buildings beforehand to protect them. First they would light one firecracker, which would light a string of them draped all around the plaza. Then with a huge explosion the Falla would begin to burn. The fire was so hot we had to back up to the curbs. The smoke became so intense we all covered our faces with our *pañuelos* in order to breathe. My eyes were tearing uncontrollably. The Valencians said they were crying because of all the emotion they felt watching their Falla burn. We Americans were crying because we hadn't slept in five days."

Salmon and Cardoon Paella

SERVES 4

1 pound salmon steak
1 Spanish laurel (bay) leaf
1/2 teaspoon pebrella
6 green peppercorns, rinsed
1/2 tablespoon Spanish sea salt
1 jar cardoons (15 ounces),
    drained, liquid reserved, sliced
    lengthwise into match sticks
6 cups water
1/4 cup olive oil
1/2 onion, chopped
4 cloves garlic, finely chopped
2 scallions (green onions)
    including green tops, sliced
2 cups Valencian rice
1/4 cup Spanish pine nuts

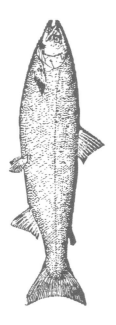

Cardoons are a relative of the artichoke and both are part of the thistle family. They require rather laborious preparation, so I use jars of the stems. The gentle flavor of the cardoons goes well with the flavor of fresh salmon. The pine nuts add texture.

1 To make the stock, trim the skin and debone the salmon, then cut into cubes. Place the trimmings in a saucepan with the laurel, pebrella, peppercorns, sea salt, the liquid from the cardoons, and the water. Bring to a boil, reduce heat, and simmer 30 minutes.

2 Pour the olive oil into a 13-inch or larger paella pan and heat. Add the onions and sauté until translucent. Add garlic and continue to cook. When the garlic is soft, stir in the scallions, pushing the vegetables to the rim of the pan, leaving the center bare. Add the cubed salmon; brown and then add cardoons.

3 Strain the fish stock and measure out 6 cups. Add this to the paella pan, and then stir in the rice and cook until done, about 20–25 minutes. While the rice is cooking, toast pine nuts in a small skillet until they start to brown. Sprinkle toasted pine nuts over the top of the rice before serving.

4 If you need to free up the stovetop, the pan can be slipped into a 350 degree F oven for the last 15 minutes of cooking.

Amontillado and Chicken Paella with Chorizo

SERVES 4

1/4 cup Spanish olive oil
4 chicken thighs
1 large onion, chopped
1 tablespoon minced garlic
2 links Spanish-style cooking
  chorizo
2 cups Spanish short-grain
  Valencian rice, preferably bomba
1 cup medium dry Amontillado
  sherry
3 cups chicken stock

Our former wine manager, James Hondros, and his wife, Amy McCray, serve Amontillado Sherry Braised Rabbit with Chorizo Bread Pudding at their restaurant, Eva. If you dine there, always ask his advice in choosing wines. Some of his wife's recipes appear later in this book, but first, here is a paella inspired by her pairing of flavors.

1 Heat the olive oil in a 12-inch paella pan and brown the chicken. Stir in the onions, sautéing until wilted, and then add the garlic, cooking another minute or two. Add the chorizo and cook until the fat is released. Then stir in the rice to coat and add the sherry. Bring to a boil. When the sherry is absorbed by the rice, add the stock, reduce the heat, and simmer until the rice is done, about 20–25 minutes.

Portuguese Spaghetti with Garlic and Cilantro

SERVES 8

1/4 cup Portuguese olive oil
6 cloves garlic, chopped
1 quart chicken stock
1 piri piri pepper or splash of Piri
  Piri Sauce (page 107), optional
3/4 cup minced cilantro leaves
1 pound angel hair pasta

This simple and quick way to cook fideo has the intense flavors I associate with Portugal.

1 Heat the oil in a 15-inch or larger paella pan and sauté garlic until golden. Add the chicken stock and piri piri and bring to a boil. Add the cilantro and pasta, and cook until the liquid is absorbed, about 3 minutes. Test a strand of pasta for doneness. If additional cooking is required, add 1/2 cup water at a time and continue to cook until done.

Piri Piri–Basted Game Hens and Cilantro-Scented Rice

SERVES 4

1/2 cup Portuguese Basting Oil (page 106), or, if you prefer a milder taste, Spanish Basting Oil (page 105)
2 game hens, split in half lengthwise
2 cloves garlic, slivered
2 tablespoons olive oil
4 cups chicken stock
3/4 cup chopped cilantro
2 cups rice

In this take-off of *arroz con pollo*, I combined two of the flavors that most remind me of Portugal: piri piri and cilantro. The cilantro-scented rice cooked on its own makes a tasty side dish.

1 Preheat oven to 350 degrees F. Brush the basting oil over the game hens and refrigerate. I like to do this in the morning of the day I plan to cook them, but busy schedules may not permit this.

2 Coat the bottom of a 12-inch or larger paella pan with basting oil and put in the split game hens.

3 Roast in the oven 30 minutes until the juice from the birds runs clear.

4 Remove them from pan and brown the garlic in the olive oil and drippings collected in the bottom of the pan. Add the chicken stock and deglaze the bottom of the pan using a wooden spatula. Add the cilantro and rice then bring to a boil.

5 When boiling, return the four game hen halves to the pan and reduce the heat. When the rice has absorbed enough water to safely move the pan, return it to the oven.

6 The total cooking time from adding the rice should be 25 minutes, stovetop and oven combined.

Garbanzo and Gamba Paella

SERVES 8

6 cloves garlic, sliced
1/4 cup olive oil
1 large can (46 ounces) clam juice
Pinch saffron
4 small dried red guindilla peppers, optional
2 pounds prawns
2 cups bomba rice
2 cups garbanzo beans, cooked
1 cup Romesco sauce (page 109)
Salt, to taste (remember that the clam juice is already salty)

This recipe marries some of my favorite flavors. The texture of the garbanzos contrasts interestingly with the rice, and the prawn-romesco combination is a flavor right out of Tarragona.

1 Sauté the garlic in olive oil in a 17-inch paella pan until it starts to brown. Add the clam juice and saffron and allow this to simmer until the liquid is suffused with color from the saffron.

2 Add the peppers and prawns, and bring to a boil. Add the rice, return to a boil, and then stir in the garbanzos, Romesco, and salt. Simmer until rice is done, about 20 minutes, adding additional liquid if needed.

Poached Pear "Paella" and Autumn Harvest Rice

SERVES 8

2 ripe pears
3 cups dry Oloroso sherry
1/2 cup raisins
1/2 cup olive oil
1 1/2 pounds pork, cubed and salted
2 cloves garlic, chopped
1 1/2 pounds chanterelle mushrooms, chopped
1 teaspoon smoked bittersweet
  pimentón
1 teaspoon Spanish sea salt
1 jar (8 ounces) piquillo pepper
  strips
3 cups water or stock plus the
  poaching liquid (6 cups in all)
1 cup wild rice
1 cup Valencian rice
1 cup fideo noodles

This paella is off the wall. A traditional Spaniard would wonder what on earth it was. So what? It tastes like an autumn day during the harvest season.

1 Peel the pears and poach them in the sherry until a fork penetrates them easily. Cool in the liquid, then remove, core, and cut into cubes, reserving liquid. Soak the raisins in some of the poaching liquid to plump them.

2 Heat olive oil in a 15-inch or larger paella pan. Brown the pork and then add the garlic, cooking until it begins to color. Stir in the mushrooms and cook until they start to absorb the oil. Sprinkle in the pimentón and salt, and then stir in the piquillo strips. Add the water and poaching liquid and bring to a boil.

3 Add the wild rice and cook 25 minutes. Then add the cubed pears, raisins, and Valencian rice and cook 10 minutes. Add the fideo and cook an additional 15 minutes, adding hot water if needed.

Pocha Beans and Clams

SERVES 6

Pinch saffron
1/2 cup dry white wine
1/2 onion, chopped
4 cloves garlic, finely chopped
1/4 cup Spanish olive oil
1 tablespoon sweet pimentón
1 dry guindilla pepper, stems
  discarded and crumbled
Pinch Spanish sea salt
1/2 cup water
2 pounds small steamer clams
4 cups cooked pochas or other
  white beans
2 tablespoons minced parsley

Is it paella if it doesn't have any rice in it? Well, this does have saffron. It is an Asturian recipe from the north coast of Spain, far from the rice fields of the southeast coast along the Mediterranean. I cook it using precooked Spanish white beans or *pochas*. Pochas are shell beans that have never been dried. They have a delicate, delicious flavor. You can use either a paella pan or a cazuela to cook this.

1 Place the saffron in a small saucepan with the wine. Heat until just below a boil, then remove from heat.

2 In a 14-inch or larger paella pan, sauté the onions and garlic in olive oil until wilted.

3 Stir in the pimentón and add the pepper, salt, water, and the saffron-wine mixture. Add the clams, shaking the pan occasionally, and cook a few minutes until clams pop open. Fold in the beans with their liquid, thinning with water if necessary. Heat through.

4 Sprinkle with parsley and serve.

Fideuá (Valencian Pasta)

SERVES 6

1 ñora dried pepper (or substitute
   ¹/₂ tablespoon pimentón)
Pinch saffron
¹/₂ cup dry white wine
1 onion, chopped
¹/₄ cup olive oil
2 cloves garlic, finely chopped
1 pound white fish such as red
   snapper, chopped into bite-size
   pieces
1 tablespoon sweet pimentón (1¹/₂
   tablespoons if not using a ñora)
1 large tomato, grated (cut tomato
   in half, shake out the seeds, and
   grate flesh, discarding skin)
5¹/₂ cups clam juice or homemade
   fish stock
1 pound fideo pasta or spaghetti
   broken into one-inch lengths
1 pound clams, cleaned

Spanish pasta, fideo, can be used in place of rice in paellas. When used this way, it is called *fideuá*, and is usually cooked in an intensely flavored fish stock so that it absorbs the flavor. The stock can be based on fish, prawns, or clams. The clams give this version a briny tang I particularly like. Fideuá is always served with Alioli (page 111), garlic mayonnaise.

1 Discarding the stem and seeds, place the ñora pepper in a small saucepan, covering with hot water. Bring to a boil and set aside to steep for half an hour.

2 Place the saffron in a separate small saucepan, add white wine and heat to just below the boiling point (microwaving for one minute works great). Set aside to steep.

3 In a 14-inch or larger paella pan, sauté the onion in the olive oil until limp. Add the garlic and continue cooking until soft. Add the fish and cook 5 minutes. Stir in the pimentón, tomatoes, and the saffron mixture, cooking for a few minutes, and then remove from heat.

4 With a mortar and pestle, or in a food processor, purée the ñora pepper with its soaking liquid. Add the cooked mixture and blend well. Measure the resulting purée, adding the clam juice or fish stock and water to make 6 cups.

5 Pour into the paella pan and bring to a boil; add pasta and then clams, hinge down. Cook until the liquid is absorbed and the clams open, about 12 minutes. It can still be soupy, as the pasta will absorb liquid during the ten minutes of dormir before serving.

Wine from Galicia

The high ridges of Bierzo produce the red wine of Galicia. The local grape is Mencia, likened to the Loire Valley Cabernet Franc. For years it was used to make low quality table and blending wines, but now there is an aggressive search throughout Spain for pockets of old vines from which big-bodied red wines can be made. Bierzo was one of the regions that benefitted from these wines coming back into style. The wines now being made there are rich and unique and still tremendous values.

Black Fideuá

SERVES 4

Pinch saffron
$^1/_2$ cup white wine, warmed
$^1/_4$ cup olive oil
1 tablespoon minced garlic
$^1/_2$ pound cleaned squid bodies,
   sliced into rings
$^1/_2$ pound fideo pasta
$^1/_2$ teaspoon sweet pimentón
2 ounces squid ink
2 tablespoons wine vinegar
1 quart clam juice
1 tablespoon minced parsley
1 cup Alioli (see page 111)

Here is a recipe for an exotic black paella dish we enjoyed at the port in Valencia. This version emerges a charcoal gray color. If you can find black pasta, you will get jet-black results.

1 Steep the saffron in the wine.

2 Heat the olive oil in a 9-inch or larger paella pan and soften the garlic. Add the squid rings and sauté briefly, 1–2 minutes. Add the pasta and sauté until lightly browned. Stir in the pimentón, followed by the squid ink, saffron-infused wine, vinegar, clam juice, and parsley. Cook until the liquid is absorbed, about 20 minutes. Serve with Alioli on the side.

Tuna with Fideo and Capers

SERVES 4

2 tablespoons olive oil
1 onion, chopped
2 to 3 cloves chopped garlic
1 can (7 ounces) Spanish tuna,
   packed in olive oil
3 tablespoons black olives, pitted
   and chopped, or 1 tablespoon
   Olivada (page 110)
1 teaspoon capers, rinsed (or more
   to taste)
$^1/_2$ cup dry white wine
$^1/_4$ teaspoon sea salt
6 cups water
$^1/_2$ pound fideo pasta
1 tablespoon minced parsley
1 lemon, juiced
Black pepper, to taste

OK. I admit it. This is only tuna noodle casserole. But it is this variation upon the theme that will amaze and delight you. Best of all, it can be on the table in 20 minutes.

1 Heat oil in a 12-inch or larger paella pan and sauté the onions and garlic until soft.

2 Add the tuna with oil and the olives and capers and sauté 1 or 2 minutes until warm. Add the wine, salt, and water, and bring to a boil. Add the pasta, returning to a boil, then reduce the heat. When the pasta has absorbed the liquid and is al dente, about 12 minutes, sprinkle with parsley, lemon juice, and a grind of fresh black pepper before serving.

Artichokes and Pasta

SERVES 4

1/2 cup Spanish olive oil
4 cloves garlic, finely chopped
1 quart vegetable stock or water
1 jar (13 ounces) artichoke hearts, drained and liquid reserved
1/2 pound fideo pasta
Salt, to taste
1 tablespoon minced parsley

Navarra grows enormous quantities of artichokes. Like cardoons, artichoke plants are thistles. Prickly and rough on the outside, their hearts are sweet and tender, perfect for this dish.

1 Heat the oil in a 12-inch paella pan and sauté garlic until soft. Add the stock and reserved artichoke juice and bring to a boil. Add the pasta. When it has absorbed the liquid and is al dente, about 12 minutes, salt to taste (there is salt in the artichoke packing liquid). Top with the artichoke hearts and cook until warmed. Sprinkle with parsley.

Wine from Navarra

Navarra grows more than premium vegetables such as artichokes. It is also a major wine-producing region. Navarra has a fairly relaxed approach to regulation of their wineries, and many French varietals are planted there. From these, I would select a bottle of Cabernet Sauvignon, but my mother would choose the barrel-fermented Chardonnay because this dish pairs just as well with red or white wine.

Salmon and Piquillo Pepper Pasta

SERVES 4

1/2 cup water
Pinch saffron
1/2 cup East India Solera Cream Sherry
1 jar (10 ounces) piquillo pepper strips marinated in olive oil and garlic
1/2 pound cooked salmon
1/2 pound pasta of choice
1/2 pint cream

The Pacific Northwest, where we live, is salmon country and I often have leftover salmon. When we do, one of my favorite ways to use it is this dish, which takes less than 30 minutes, start to finish.

1 Put water in a 12-inch or larger paella pan with the saffron threads. Heat until hot. Add the sherry, pepper strips with the marinating oil, and salmon. Bring to a boil.

2 Add the pasta and cook until the liquid is absorbed, about 12 minutes. Test the pasta; it should be al dente. Stir in the cream and cook an additional minute or 2 until incorporated.

Saffron Pasta Con Queso Manchego

SERVES 4

1 quart chicken stock
Small pinch saffron (12 to 15 threads)
Pinch salt
1/2 pound fideo or other pasta
2 tablespoons minced parsley
1 cup shredded Manchego
12 slices hard-cured chorizo or cooked linguiça, optional

Think of this satisfying dish as macaroni and cheese for grown-ups.

1 Pour the chicken stock into a 12-inch or larger paella pan, add the saffron and bring to a boil. The amount of saffron you use should depend on how much you like it and how fresh your supply is. Sniff the jar to determine the latter; go light the first time you make this recipe until you determine the former.

2 Add the salt and then the pasta, stirring occasionally, and cook until it is al dente and most of the liquid has been absorbed, about 12 minutes for most pasta. Stir in the parsley and cheese; heat until it melts.

3 For meat lovers, place very thin slices of chorizo or cooked linguiça on top and run the pan under the broiler until the surface starts to brown.

Fideo Pasta with Seafood in Oloroso Cream Sauce

SERVES 4

2 tablespoons olive oil
1 tablespoon garlic, finely chopped
1 pound smoked or cooked salmon, flaked, and/or shrimp meat or crab
1/2 cup dry Oloroso sherry
3 cups clam juice or water
1/2 pound fideo pasta
1 cup half-and-half or cream
1 tablespoon minced parsley

The rich, woodsy taste of smoked salmon marries with the oak-aged dry Oloroso sherry in this opulent sauce. You don't really taste the garlic; it just adds an underlying complexity to the salmon-dominated sauce with the subtle hint of sherry expanding the theme. The salmon is usually salty enough that you won't need to add any additional seasoning. If using fresh salmon, add 1/2 teaspoon Spanish sea salt with the water. You can substitute orzo if fideo is unavailable. The Spanish and Portuguese mix seafood, not just in paella, but throughout their cuisine. So feel free to combine salmon, shrimp, and crab in this dish.

1 Heat oil in a 12-inch or larger paella pan and cook the garlic until soft. Add the seafood, heating through but avoiding scorching. When hot, add the sherry and clam juice, then bring to a boil.

2 Add the pasta and return to a boil. Reduce the heat and cook until the pasta has absorbed the liquid and is al dente, about 10–12 minutes. Add the half-and-half and parsley and cook an additional minute or 2 until incorporated.

Covered Terracotta Cookware

Cazuelas, Cocotes, and Ollas

The terracotta cazuela was one of the original cooking vessels developed throughout the world. When you cook in terracotta, you cook as a Roman would have cooked, as a pre-Roman cooked, as a pre-bronze-age cave dweller cooked.

Spanish cazuelas have become the workhorse of our kitchen because they are so versatile. They can be used with direct heat on a burner, so they can be used to sauté onions and garlic in olive oil or to reduce tomatoes and peppers to a sofrito. Then they can be slid into the oven to finish whatever dish you are preparing, leaving you free to make the salad while it bakes. I use our largest cazuela every Thanksgiving to roast our turkey, a turkey basted with a touch of Spain (page 205). When it is time to serve, the cazuela is attractive enough that it can be brought right to the table. They hold heat very well, so cazuelas are also great for transporting food to a potluck. And they wash easily. When something gets baked onto the surface, I find that just soaking the cazuela overnight makes it easy to clean.

Recipes for Terracotta Cookware

Artichoke Soup

SERVES 4–6

3 cloves garlic, split in half
2 tablespoons olive oil
1 large jar (13 ounces) artichoke
   hearts, drained
2 cups vegetable stock
Pinch salt
1 cup whole milk
1 tablespoon extra virgin olive oil

Navarra grows and cans thousands and thousands of artichoke hearts every year. This soup can be adapted to any vegetable. Just substitute a cup of cooked vegetables for the jarred artichoke hearts.

1 Sauté the garlic in the oil in a medium olla until soft and remove to a blender with a slotted spoon. Purée the garlic and the artichoke hearts, slowly adding vegetable stock until smooth. Return to the olla and heat to the boiling point. Salt to taste, then reduce heat and stir in milk.

2 As it is served, drizzle a little olive oil over each bowl in a cute spiral. Use a really fruity Spanish extra virgin olive oil.

Cardoon and Potato Soup

SERVES 2–4

2 large potatoes, quartered
1 jar (14 ounces) cardoons
Pinch Spanish sea salt
Black pepper, to taste
Drizzle Spanish extra virgin
   olive oil

Potatoes provide a perfect foil for the subtle flavor of the cardoons, letting them shine through like sun rays through clouds.

1 Place the potato pieces in a medium olla, cover with salted water and cook until tender. Reserve the cooking water.

2 In a blender, purée potatoes and cardoons, thinning with the water the potatoes were cooked in until it resembles heavy cream. Return to the olla and heat just to boiling. Taste and add salt and pepper.

3 After placing in serving bowls, artistically drizzle a healthy amount of olive oil over the top.

Portuguese Bean Soup

SERVES 6

4 tablespoons olive oil, preferably Portuguese, divided
4 cloves garlic, chopped
1 onion, chopped
3 cups cooked red beans, divided
3 cups beef stock, divided
1/2 cup diced linguiça (Portuguese sausage)
3 tablespoons Pimenta Moída (page 105)
2 tablespoons Tomate Frito (page 104)
Pinch salt

Angela do Mar has worked in our Seattle deli for years. On winter days she always makes a hot soup. When I asked her for this recipe, she groaned. "You'll want measurements." I knew what she meant but I had to agree. So she cheerfully dug around for a measuring cup and a tablespoon and wrote this down. Usually, she just starts tossing stuff in a pot and then after a while she tastes it to see how she is doing. ◡ Pimenta Moída is a wonderful crushed red pepper sauce from the Portuguese Azore Islands that adds a distinct flavor to anything from stew to scrambled eggs.

1 Heat 2 tablespoons of the olive oil in a medium olla and sauté the garlic and onion. Add 2 cups of the beans and 1 cup of the beef stock, and simmer 20 minutes. Remove to a blender and purée until smooth.

2 Wipe out the olla and then add the remaining olive oil and linguiça, cooking until the sausage sweats fat. Add the purée, remaining beef stock, and remaining cup of beans.

3 Season with Pimenta Moída, Tomate Frito, and salt, adjusting quantities to taste.

Wine from Douro

Portugal is known for making big, earthy red wines. The gorge of the Douro River is planted with grapes for making port, but recently many of them are now also being used to make red table wines. The grape with the most nobility is the Touriga Nacional, but there are several other varieties in the Douro blend. Look for wines from the port lodges and prepare to be pleasantly surprised at how good they have become in the hands of contemporary winemakers.

Fish in Garlic Saffron Sauce

SERVES 2

¹/₄ cup olive oil
4 cloves garlic
Pinch saffron
1 pound firm fillets of a white fish
4 tablespoons
¹/₂ cup dry white wine
6 white asparagus spears, optional
1 tablespoon minced parsley for
  garnish

While we may not have Spain's rich maritime larder of Mediterranean seafood, our local waters produce an abundance of alternatives. A cazuela is great for cooking fish dishes because it goes from stove top to oven to table. The fillets of any firm fish that will not fall apart when cooked will work. I prefer halibut, but I have even done this recipe with salmon.

1 Preheat oven to 350 degrees F.

2 While the oven is warming, heat oil in a medium cazuela until a haze forms. Brown the garlic, being careful it does not burn, but be sure it is golden brown as that will be the essential flavor in the sauce. Remove to a mortar, add saffron, and use the pestle to grind to a paste while the fish browns.

3 Dust the fish with flour, shaking off excess. Fry in the same oil used to cook the garlic, turning when browned. When browned on both sides, remove to a platter.

4 Deglaze the cazuela with the wine, then add the garlic-saffron paste and the fish, and place the asparagus spears along the sides. Bake 20 minutes. Sprinkle with minced parsley and serve.

Salmon and Lentils

SERVES 4

¹/₄ cup olive oil
4 cloves garlic, sliced
1 large onion, chopped
2 cups cooked Pardina lentils
2 pounds salmon, divided into four
  portions, either steaks or fillets
Pinch sweet pimentón
1 tablespoon parsley, minced

Angela do Mar's son, Nuno, was for many years a commercial fisherman in Alaska. Every voyage, he hand selected a few perfect salmon to ship to his mother. One time she gave me a huge, perfect fish that I divided in any number of ways. This was my favorite.

1 Preheat oven to 350 degrees F.

2 Heat oil in a medium cazuela, add garlic slices, and cook until golden brown. Remove garlic and reserve. Add the chopped onion, cook until soft, and add lentils, stirring to combine. Place salmon portions on the lentils, topping with the golden garlic slices and dust with pimentón. Bake until the fish is cooked, approximately 15 minutes, depending on the thickness of fillets. Sprinkle with parsley and serve.

Piquillo Peppers Stuffed with Ground Turkey Picada

MAKES 18 TAPAS OR 9 SERVINGS

1/4 cup olive oil
1/2 pound ground turkey
1 cup Picada (page 108)
4 tablespoons Amontillado sherry, divided
1 cup White Sauce (page 112)
1 tin (10 ounces, 18 whole) piquillo peppers, juice reserved
Warm water to thin as needed

There are cows in the north of Spain and a tradition of eating beef. Else-where in Spain, the steak you eat probably came of age in Argentina from where it was exported to Spain. In the north, they like to stuff piquillos with a picada of ground beef. I find the flavor quite intense. Here, I have substituted ground turkey.

1 Preheat oven to 350 degrees F.

2 Heat the olive oil in an 8-inch cazuela and cook the ground turkey, breaking it apart with a spatula as it cooks so that it crumbles. Add the Picada, stirring well. Moisten with 2 tablespoons of the sherry. Remove from the cazuela.

3 While this cools, use a medium saucepan to make the White Sauce.

4 Using a small spoon, fill the peppers with the turkey mixture and fan out in a circle in the cazuela, points towards the center. Add the juice of the piquillos and the sherry to the White Sauce; then, if necessary, use a very warm water to thin it to the consistency of heavy cream. Pour over the peppers in the cazuela and bake 20 minutes.

Piglet

Piglet was my target meal on our first trip to Spain. I had chosen to re-read Hemingway's *The Sun Also Rises* on the flight over and had emerged from the plane with a Hemingway agenda for seeing Madrid. We attended our first bull-fight, and afterward we went to Casa Botín, the 250-year-old res-taurant below the Plaza Major on Calle de Cuchilleros.

On the way to our table at Botín, we stopped to inspect the tiled alcove where the suckling pigs are roasted in a blazing wood oven. They sit on a shelf there, side by side, in a neat row, a line of tiny faces staring out of the terracotta cazuelas they are roasted in. For more than two hundred years, a row of little pigs has always waited on these shelves to be served to hungry travelers.

Sanlúcar French Fries

PER SERVING

A heaping mound of thin-cut french fries cooked in olive oil and salted

TOPPING PER SERVING
1/4 cup olive oil
2 cloves garlic, sliced
2 tablespoons roughly diced jamón
1/4 pound Dover sole fillets
2 tablespoons dry Oloroso sherry
Dusting of sea salt

Oh, gosh, this version of french fries is so Spanish. We ate it standing at the bar in Casa Bigote. The man standing at the bar next to us was eating this dish. We asked the waiter what it was and before we knew it, we were eating one also. We had no intention of eating it all, just tasting it, but we licked the plate clean.

1 Heat oil in an 8-inch cazuela until it hazes, and then add garlic slices and brown. Remove the garlic with a slotted spoon when it is golden and reserve. Stir in the jamón and add the fish fillets. When the fish is browned on one side, flip and brown the other side.

2 Pile the fries on a plate and top with the fish and jamón. Return the garlic to pan with sherry and deglaze. Pour over the fish and dust with sea salt.

3 Accompany with a glass of fresh Manzanilla sherry chilled icy cold.

Manzanilla Sherry

Manzanilla sherry is only made in Sanlúcar de Barrameda where the breezes stir the air in the bodegas enough to keep the *flor* alive year-round. The bodegas are huge, filled with old barrels and with dirt floors that are sprinkled with water in the afternoons to keep the humidity high. Eventually, sherry barrels find their way to Scotland where they are used to age Scotch, which takes on some of the subtle aromas of the wines absorbed over the years by the oak wood.

Salmon Fillet Glazed with Pedro Ximénez

SERVES 2

1/2 tablespoon minced garlic
2 tablespoons olive oil
1/2 cup Pedro Ximénez Montilla
2 (1/2-pound) salmon fillets

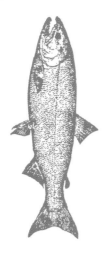

Pedro Ximénez (PX) is a sweet Montilla, which is what sherry is called when it is from Córdoba rather than Jerez. In this wine country around Córdoba, dry sunny conditions are perfect for drying grapes on mesh mats laid down on slopes facing the sun, a process called *tendiendas*. Only after the grapes are raisinated are they are taken to the bodegas to be made into sweet wine. The concentration of flavor is intense. The sweetness of the PX in this marinade compliments the natural oils of the salmon.

1 Using a 10-inch cazuela, slowly sauté minced garlic in olive oil over low heat until soft. Increase heat, add Pedro Ximénez, and reduce by half. Remove from heat and use a brush to coat salmon fillets with the reduced sauce.

2 Bake at 350 degrees F until fork tender or broil fillets until fork tender and serve.

Halibut with Prawns in Romesco

SERVES 4

1/4 cup olive oil
1 clove garlic, sliced
1 pound halibut
2 tablespoons flour
1 pound prawns or clams
1 cup dry white wine if using prawns, 1/2 cup if using clams because they release nectar as they cook
1 cup Romesco (page 109)

Pairing seafood is a Spanish culinary custom. White fish is often cooked in a cazuela with either clams or prawns. A rich blend of nuts, red ñora peppers, and bread, Romesco makes a rich sauce that plays perfectly off the briny seafood.

1 Preheat oven to 350 degrees F. Heat oil in a medium cazuela until a haze forms, then add the garlic and brown. When the garlic is golden, remove with a slotted spoon and reserve.

3 Dust halibut with flour. Place in the hot oil, skin side up, and fry until brown, about 5 minutes, and then turn over. If using prawns, slide them on either side of halibut and cook an additional 5 minutes, flipping prawns when they start to turn pink. Add reserved garlic and white wine. Stir in Romesco.

4 If using clams, cook halibut for the first 5 minutes then add clams, garlic, white wine, and Romesco. Bring to a boil.

5 Slide cazuela into the oven and bake 20 minutes. Test halibut by probing gently with a fork to see if the center is cooked to your taste.

Lemon Scallops with Amontillado Sherry

SERVES 2

2 cloves garlic, minced
2 tablespoons olive oil
1/2 cup flour
Pinch salt
Pinch pepper
1 pound sea scallops
1 Meyer lemon, zest and juice
1/4 cup Amontillado sherry

Lush lemon trees grow in Spain, their branches decorated with the tell-tale oblongs of fruit, deep green when immature, then lightening to lemon yellow. The Amontillado and the lemon juice balance each other out. Amontillado has a range from very dry to slightly sweet. If you can not get a Meyer lemon and use the tarter variety, be sure to use a medium, rather than dry, Amontillado or, in a pinch, add a pinch of brown sugar.

1 Using a 10-inch cazuela, sauté the garlic in oil until soft.

2 Mix together the flour, salt, and pepper, and then lightly dust the scallops. Add to the garlic and sauté another 2 minutes without stirring. Sprinkle the lemon zest on top, turn the scallops over, and cook an additional 2 minutes, then add the sherry. Remove the scallops with a slotted spoon to a heated serving plate. Deglaze the cazuela with lemon juice, reducing liquid by half, and drizzle over scallops.

Garbanzos à la Catalana

SERVES 4

1/4 cup olive oil
1 large onion, chopped
1/4 pound butifarra sausage, sliced
2 tablespoons jamón serrano ham, diced
1 cup Tomate Frito (page 104)
1 teaspoon sea salt
1 bay leaf
1/4 teaspoon black pepper
4 cups cooked garbanzo beans, drained
1 tablespoon minced parsley

Garbanzos have been grown in the Mediterranean forever. What makes these Catalan is the butifarra, a white sausage.

1 In a large olla, heat the oil and then sauté the onion, sausage, and ham until the onion is soft. Add the Tomate Frito, salt, bay leaf, and pepper. Cook slowly, covered, about 15 minutes. Add the garbanzos, cover, and cook another 20 minutes. Sprinkle with parsley and serve.

White Bean Shellfish Stew

SERVES 6

1/2 cup olive oil
4 cloves garlic, finely chopped
1 onion, chopped
1 pound prawns
1 tablespoon pimentón
1 bay leaf
1 cup Tomate Frito (page 104)
1/2 cup dry white wine
1 pound squid
3 cups cooked white beans
3 baby lobsters, cut in half
1 lemon, juiced
1/4 cup minced parsley

This is my version of a dish I enjoyed so much in Cabo Verde. It is one of those things where you use what your fishmonger has to offer the day you are shopping. So substitute other shellfish freely.

1 Heat the oil in a large olla. Add the garlic and cook 1 minute until softened.

2 Add the onion and cook an additional 5 minutes until translucent. Add the prawns and toss to coat in oil. When they turn pink, stir in the pimentón and add the bay leaf. Add the Tomate Frito and white wine, and bring to a boil. Stir in the squid and cover and cook until the squid is tender, approximately 20 minutes. Stir in the beans, and then arrange the lobster halves on top. Drizzle with lemon juice and sprinkle with parsley. Cover and simmer until all ingredients are hot.

Pork Tenderloin with Amontillado Sherry and Chestnuts

SERVES 2

2 ounces Amontillado sherry
1 tablespoon chopped purple garlic
1 Spanish bay leaf
1 (3/4-pound) pork tenderloin
2 tablespoons Spanish olive oil
1/2 teaspoon sweet pimentón
1/2 cup Spanish chestnuts

Amontillado sherry is the color of a golden autumn leaf and tastes of honey and nuts. Here I pair it with chestnuts to create a perfect autumn evening dish.

1 Mix the sherry, garlic, and bay leaf, and marinate the pork tenderloin in this mixture at least 2 hours and up to 24 hours.

2 Preheat oven to 350 degrees F.

3 Place tenderloin and marinade in a medium cazuela that has been brushed with the olive oil. Roast the meat until the internal temperature is 160 degrees F (about an hour), basting every 20 minutes, adding a small amount of water if necessary. Remove the meat from the cazuela.

4 Add the pimentón to juices in the cazuela, stirring to blend. Add the chestnuts and toss.

5 Slice the meat and return to the cazuela, coating well with juices, and then serve.

Halibut Baked on a Bed of White Beans

SERVES 4

1/4 cup olive oil
4 cloves garlic, sliced
1 large ripe tomato, chopped and seeds discarded
2 cups cooked white beans
2 pounds halibut fillet, divided into four portions
Pinch sweet pimentón

People do not always think of mixing beans or lentils with seafood, but they should. These savory combinations are at once both familiar to the palate and freshly new. It takes fish, often thought of as a light meal, and turns it into hearty comfort food. This one places halibut in bed with beans, and it is simple and quick to prepare.

1 Preheat oven to 350 degrees F.

2 Heat oil in a medium cazuela, add garlic, and cook until golden brown.

3 Remove garlic and reserve. Add chopped tomato, stir, and add beans, stirring to combine.

4 Place halibut fillets on the beans, topping with the golden garlic slices, and dust with pimentón. Bake until the halibut is cooked, approximately 15 minutes, depending on the thickness of the fillets.

Rosado

This dish begs for a glass of *rosado*. In addition to making excellent red and white wines, Navarra is well known for its rosados, dry rosé wines. If you visit Spain and happen to be dining on a patio at lunch time, you will see bottles of chilled rosados on many of the tables. Rosé wines have a mixed reputation in the United States, where many were vinified off-dry with some residual sugars that gave them a reputation among wine snobs as being no better than soda pop. But Spanish rosados are very dry and refreshing.

Pork and Potatoes Stewed with Smoked Paprika

SERVES 12

4 pounds pork shoulder or other cut
1/2 bottle (375 milliliters) dry red wine
12 cloves garlic, 6 crushed, 6 finely chopped, divided
4 bay leaves
4 tablespoons smoked paprika (since you may not be cooking this over a wood fire, the La Vera smoked paprika lends authentic aromas), divided
1 cup olive oil
1 onion, roughly chopped
1 teaspoon cumin, preferably seeds just crushed in your yellow mortar
Pinch salt
6 potatoes, cut into chunks
2 cups cooked garbanzo beans

This is a great one-dish meal cooked in a cazuela. You can make a little or a lot; go heavy on the seasoning or light. It is the type of dish that was traditionally cooked by field hands over grapevine pruning in the vineyards, and you can imagine that opinions and ingredients varied.

1 Marinate pork in enough red wine to cover, seasoned with the crushed cloves of garlic, the bay leaves, and 2 tablespoons paprika for at least a day.

2 Drain the pork, reserving the marinade, and cut into cubes.

3 Heat the oil in a large cazuela, add pork cubes and brown. Add the onion and the chopped garlic, and sauté until cooked. Stir in the cumin, salt, and the remaining paprika and cook for a minute, then add the reserved marinade and the potatoes and/or the cooked garbanzo beans. Cook until the potatoes are soft.

4 I usually do this in a hot (450 degrees) convection oven, leaving it in for 20–30 minutes, but it works just as well on the stove top.

Lentils with Portuguese Sausage and Red Finger Peppers

SERVES 4

1 tablespoon olive oil
1/4 pound linguiça, diced
1 tablespoon finely chopped garlic
1 tablespoon bittersweet pimentón
4 cups cooked Pardina lentils
1 bay leaf
1/4 cup Tomate Frito (page 104)
2 large red finger peppers, rinsed, seeded, and chopped into 1/4-inch squares

One summer we took these lentils to every potluck we were invited to. We always took the dish home empty. While there were innumerable pasta salads, we were always the only people to bring lentils, and they were always a hit.

1 In a 10-inch cazuela, heat the oil and brown the linguiça until crisp. Add the garlic and cook until soft. Stir in the pimentón and add the lentils, bay leaf, and Tomate Frito.

2 Heat until the mixture bubbles, stirring constantly, and thinning with water if needed. Stir in the peppers and serve.

Tolosana Beans with Two Embutidos

SERVES 2

1/4 pound butifarra, chopped into small bits
1/4 pound Basque-style chorizo, chopped into small bits
1/2 medium onion, chopped
1 tablespoon finely chopped garlic
1 tablespoon sweet pimentón
2 cups Tolosana red beans, or other cooked red bean of choice

This is a Basque and Catalan wedding. The red beans are named for the village in the Basque Country where they originated; the white sausage is Catalan. This dish has the classic Spanish combination of a white sausage and a red one. If you like morcilla, use that rather than the Basque chorizo.

1 In a 10-inch cazuela, brown the butifarra and chorizo bits until crisp. Add the onion and cook until soft. Add the garlic and cook until the aroma fills the kitchen and then stir in the pimentón. Add the beans and bring to a boil, reduce heat, and simmer until flavors meld, 5–10 minutes.

Swiss Chard and Lentils

SERVES 4 AS SIDE DISH

1 bunch fresh Swiss chard
2 cups chicken stock
1 cup Pardina lentils
1 tablespoon raisins
1 tablespoon pine nuts, toasted

In Portugal and Galicia, the climate is cool and winter greens such as Swiss chard play an important role in the cuisine. The simplest way to fancy them up is to add some toasted pine nuts and some rehydrated raisins. Here is a dish that combines them with a legume. European lentils cook quickly unless they are old, in which case, they should be soaked like beans.

1 Wash the chard, cut up stems, and chop the leaves, keeping the stems and leaves separated.

2 Pour the chicken stock into a medium cazuela and add the lentils and raisins. If using fresh chard, add the stems and bring to a boil.

3 When the lentils have cooked for 20–30 minutes, add the chard leaves. Cook until heated through, sprinkle with pine nuts, and serve.

VARIATION For an even faster preparation, you can also use precooked Pardina lentils. Just combine the lentils and chard in cazuela and heat.

White Beans with Brotes

SERVES 4 AS SIDE DISH

2 cups cooked white beans
1 cup brotes (garlic shoots)
2 tablespoons Spanish extra virgin
   olive oil
1/4 teaspoon Spanish coarse
   ground sea salt
2 tablespoons Pimentón Bread
   Crumbs (page 122)

On one of our spring visits, the farmers' markets in Murcia were full of green garlic shoots—brotes—and we found them being cooked with everything that trip, from adding them to steamed clams to tossing them in with squid cooked in its own ink. Here, the color of the white beans contrasts charmingly with the green garlic shoots, and the subtle flavor is divine.

1 Preheat broiler.

2 Place the beans and garlic shoots in a 10-inch cazuela. Stirring gently, heat to the boiling point on a stove-top burner, adding liquid to the beans and brotes as needed. Splash the surface with olive oil and sprinkle on sea salt and bread crumbs. Broil until the surface caramelizes (browns).

Portuguese White Beans with Linguiça

SERVES 6

1 onion, chopped
2 cloves garlic, finely chopped
4 tablespoons Portuguese olive oil
1 pound linguiça, sliced
1 1/2 teaspoons bittersweet
   pimentón.
2 tablespoons Pimenta Moída
   (page 105)
1/4 cup Tomate Frito (page 104)
1 tablespoon white wine vinegar
4 cups cooked white beans

The flavors in this thick bean stew are far more complex than its simple title.

1 In a large cazuela or olla, sauté the onion and garlic in oil until limp. Add the linguiça and cook until heated through. Stir in the pimentón, then add the Pimenta Moída, Tomate Frito, vinegar, and beans. Simmer at least 20 minutes before serving.

Roast Saffron Chicken

SERVES 4

4 cloves garlic, finely chopped
1 bay leaf
1 teaspoon Spanish sea salt
1 pinch saffron threads
1 tablespoon Spanish sweet
  pimentón
1/2 cup Spanish olive oil
1 large, whole chicken
1 orange or lemon, quartered

This results in a moist chicken with a crisp, colorful, golden yellow skin and a wonderful Spanish aroma. There is very little preparation time and it needs virtually no attention while roasting except basting once or twice.

1 Preheat oven to 450 degrees F.

2 Using a mortar and pestle, crush the garlic, bay leaf, salt, and saffron until they form a paste, then incorporate the pimentón, and then the oil. Brush this mixture over the exterior of the chicken and push the orange quarters into the body cavity.

3 Roast in a cazuela large enough to hold the chicken until done, approximately 40 minutes.

Catalan Chicken à la Sidra

SERVES 4

1/4 cup Spanish olive oil
1 chicken, cut in pieces and dusted
  with salt and pepper
2 large onions, chopped
1/2 pound wild mushrooms such as
  chanterelles, sliced
1 cup Picada (page 108)
1 bottle (750 milliliter) sidra
  (sparkling apple cider from
  Asturias in Northern Spain)
1 baguette, sliced and toasted

The recipe, which combines all the great fall flavors—apples, nuts, and wild mushrooms—was in one of our newsletters and we have customers who still cook it every autumn when the leaves start to turn.

1 Cover the bottom of a large cazuela with oil and brown the chicken. Remove the chicken to a warm platter. Remove any excess fat that accumulated in the pan.

2 Add the onions and reduce the heat, slowly cooking them down to a sofrito (almost a paste). Be patient. Add the mushrooms and cook, adding olive oil if necessary and increasing the heat. When the mushrooms are cooked, stir in the Picada and return the chicken to the cazuela, adding the sidra to cover (in our cazuela, this takes the entire bottle). Cook 45 minutes. Top with slices of baguette.

Portuguese Chicken

SERVES 4

1 tablespoon course sea salt
4 cloves garlic, chopped
1 tablespoon hot smoked pimentón
¼ cup Piri Piri Sauce (page 107)
¼ cup olive oil
1 chicken, cut into halves or
  quarters

It is appropriate that I associate this dish so closely with Portugal because the folk art symbol of Portugal is a chicken, and chickens, or, more properly, roosters, are everywhere.

1 Put the salt in a mortar and add garlic. Mash together, then grind in pimentón.

2 Add in the Piri Piri Sauce followed by the olive oil. You should now have a nice paste. Using a brush, coat the chicken on all sides.

3 Refrigerate 24 hours, then grill or bake at 450 degrees F for 45–60 minutes.

Wines from Alentejo

Much of the Alentejo in southern Portugal is rural farmland with all the economic problems associated with farming in a dry climate. When we first visited there in the 1980s, it was still common to see animals being used to work the fields in scenes right out of the Middle Ages.

The wines of the Alentejo, many made from the Periquita grape, are inexpensive and delicious. They always remind me of honest, humble people with hands rough from working their fields enjoying a tumbler of wine with neighbors at day's end.

The Cataplana

Cataplanas are hinged, domed pans that clamp closed to seal in moisture. As a result, no liquid needs to be added and clams can cook in their own juice, but this does not prohibit you from adding a splash of wine if you want. Vinho Verde, because it has low alcohol, is a good choice of wine for using in a cataplana.

When the cooking is done, pull the pin, remove the lid, and serve right in the pan. There are cork pads with a depression designed to put under a cataplana when it is put on the table. The round wooden platters for *pulpo* can also be put to work here.

Sometimes people use a wok stand with their cataplana. We find that they are steady enough to place directly on the burner of either a gas or electric range. On an electric range, the bottom of the pan should be in contact with the burner. We sauté right in the pan before clamping it shut.

Recipes for the Cataplana

Traditional Clams Cataplana

SERVES 4

1 onion, thinly sliced
1 green bell pepper, thinly sliced
4 tablespoons Portuguese olive oil
1 bay leaf
6 ounces jamón, roughly diced
6 ounces linguiça and/or chouriço
   sausage, diced
1 tomato, chopped
Pinch pimentón
Dash Piri Piri Sauce (page 107)
3 pounds clams, scrubbed and
   ready to cook
2 tablespoons minced parsley

The combination of pork with clams may have developed during the inquisition to expose Jews and Muslims who could eat neither shellfish nor pork. However sinister the original intention may or may not have been, the juxtaposition of these flavors was fortuitous. This has become Portugal's signature dish just as paella has become Spain's.

1 With the cataplana open, sauté the onion and bell pepper in the olive oil with the bay leaf.

2 Cook until the onion is translucent and then add the jamón and the linguiça and heat through. Add the tomato and stir in the pimentón. Add the Piri Piri Sauce and the clams, and then sprinkle with the parsley. Close the cataplana and cook over medium heat 10 minutes.

3 Open the cataplana and serve with a chewy, crusty bread for dipping and a glass of chilled Vinho Verde wine.

Wine from Vinho Verde

Vinho Verde, literally "green wine" is from the north of Portugal, close to its border with Galicia. It is a refreshing white wine that is low in alcohol and, if fresh with a slight spritz, has just the barest hint of tiny bubbles. Ordinary Vinho Verde is inexpensive, but there are versions made with the *Alvarinho* grape (Albariño across the Minho River in Galicia), which are pricier.

Clams with Cilantro

SERVES 2

1/4 cup Portuguese olive oil
4 cloves garlic, sliced
1 pound fresh clams, scrubbed and
   ready to cook
1/4 cup chopped cilantro leaves,
   divided

I first had this lighter version of clams cataplana in a sidewalk café in Faro, the busy port and political center of the Algarve. The Algarve, the southern coast of Portugal, is a destination for beach tourism. It is also where the cataplana originated.

1 Using a cataplana, heat the olive oil over medium-high heat. Stir in the garlic and brown, being careful not to burn. Add the clams and half of the cilantro, and then clamp down the lid. Cook until the clams are done, about 9 minutes, giving the pan a couple of little shakes to distribute the juices (some of my Portuguese customers actually flip the pan over, but be careful as they might leak some moisture).

2 Open the cataplana by removing the hinge pin and top. Sprinkle the remaining cilantro over the clams and serve in the cataplana.

Clams with Smoked Pimentón

SERVES 4

1 onion, diced
1/4 cup Portuguese olive oil
1 teaspoon garlic, finely chopped
2 teaspoons La Vera smoked sweet
   pimentón
1/4 cup minced parsley
1/2 cup Manzanilla or Fino sherry
3 pounds steamer clams, scrubbed
1 lemon, quartered

The aroma of smoldering oak from the pimentón infuses this dish, which is further enriched with Manzanilla sherry and garlic.

1 Using an 11-inch cataplana, cook the onion in oil over medium heat until mushy.

2 Stir in the garlic and cook another couple of minutes. Stir in the pimentón and cook 1 minute. By now, you should have a nice *sofrito*. Add the parsley and the sherry and bring to a boil. Add the clams and cover. Cook until all the clams open, about 9 minutes.

3 Sprinkle with a squeeze of fresh lemon.

4 If the cook did not drink it, you should still have some sherry to sip as you eat the clams and sop up the broth with bread. If not, open another bottle.

Clams Madeira

In this dish, the flavor of the wine combines with the flavor of the caramelized pork to make a rich and heady sauce for the clams.

SERVES 6

1/4 cup olive oil, preferably from Portugal
1 pound lean pork, cut into cubes
4 cloves garlic, finely chopped
1/2 cup Madeira
2 pounds small clams, scrubbed and ready to cook

1 Heat the oil in a large cataplana and add the pork. When it is very brown on one side, turn and add the garlic. Continue cooking, tossing occasionally so the ingredients cook evenly, until the garlic is golden. Do not allow the garlic to blacken. Add the Madeira, toss, and add the clams. Toss again and clamp the cataplana shut. Cook another 7–9 minutes.

2 It is best to open the cataplana right at the table so your guests can be suffused in the rich aromas. Be sure to serve some bread for dipping in the sauce.

Madeira

Madeira is a little piece of Portugal, an island, five hundred miles from Lisbon in the Atlantic and one hundred miles west of Morocco. Its rain-drenched volcanic soils produce a dazzling array of flowers and fruits as well as a unique family of fortified wines ranging from off dry to sweet, but in every case, the sweetness of the wine is off-set by its natural acidity.

Clams and Morels

Pairing clams with mushrooms and fortified wine is something I first experienced in Seville as a tapa at the bar in Casa Robles. They do this same pairing with baby shrimp. Of course, they use Fino sherry, but this is a Portuguese cataplana recipe and Madeira really enhances the mushroom flavor.

SERVES 6

1/4 cup full flavored olive oil from Portugal
4 cloves garlic, sliced
1 pound morel or other flavorful mushrooms, sliced
1/2 cup Madeira wine (Rainwater or Bual)
4 pounds small clams, scrubbed and ready to cook

1 Heat oil in the bottom half of a large cataplana. Cook the garlic until it just begins to turn a golden color. Add the mushrooms and cook until soft. Add the wine and heat. Stir the clams into the mushrooms and clamp the top of the cataplana closed. Cook over medium-high heat about 9 minutes.

2 Check to see if all the clams are open. Lightly toss them to distribute the mushrooms and serve.

Prawns and Romesco

SERVES 4

1 cup Romesco Sauce (page 109)
2 pounds prawns

The combination of prawns and Romesco is traditional. The results are finger-licking good. This is also great served as a tapa.

1 Heat the Romesco in a large cataplana, thinning it with a little water, if necessary, to the consistency of heavy cream. Add the prawns and toss to coat. Cover the cataplana and clamp shut. Cook over medium heat until the prawns are cooked through, about 10 minutes. Toss prawns again and serve.

Mussels in Picada and Tawny Port

SERVES 4

1/4 cup tawny port
1 cup Picada (page 108)
2 pounds mussels, washed and de-bearded
1 tablespoon minced parsley

Galicia, along the northwest coast of Spain above Portugal, is green and lush and resembles the Pacific Northwest. The bays of Galicia are filled with anchored rafts of eucalyptus logs beneath which hang ropes that act as mussel nurseries. When mature, the mussels are harvested and rushed to seafood markets across Spain on overnight trucks. A day late and they are just a memory. Here is a quick way to make your next mussels memorable. This works equally well with mussels or clams. The shellfish is tasty, the sauce is ambrosia.

1 Heat the port in a large cataplana, stirring in Picada. Add the mussels, sprinkle with the parsley, and clamp the top shut. Cook 5–10 minutes until all the shellfish open.

Clams and Green Garlic

SERVES 4

1 tablespoon extra virgin olive oil
1 jar (10 ounces) brotes (green garlic shoots)
3 pounds small clams, scrubbed

Clams are like a blank canvas. They invite seasoning, subtle and robust. Brotes are subtle.

1 Heat the oil in a cataplana. Add the brotes and heat through. Stir in clams.

2 Clamp the cataplana shut and cook until all clams are open, about 9 minutes.

Azorean Beef with Peppers

SERVES 2

2 strips bacon, diced
1 pound beef steak, cubed
$1/2$ medium onion, chopped
2 cloves garlic, chopped
$1/2$ green bell pepper, coarsely chopped
$1/2$ red bell pepper, coarsely chopped
2 tablespoons tawny port
$1/4$ cup Pimenta Moída (page 105)
1 tablespoon parsley, chopped

The cataplana can be used first as a wok, to stir-fry things, and then clamped shut to steam them, melding their flavors and keeping them moist. This is exactly what we have done in this recipe. Pimenta Moída contains ample salt, so don't just reflexively add more.

1 In a medium cataplana, slowly heat the bacon to release the fat, then increase heat and brown. Add the beef and brown 5 minutes. Add the onion and garlic and wilt, about 5 minutes. Add the bell peppers and cook until soft, approximately 5 minutes. Stir in the tawny port, Pimenta Moída, and parsley. Close the cataplana and cook until flavors meld, about 10 minutes.

2 Serve with a little Pimenta Moída on the side.

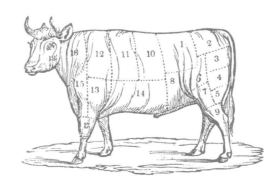

Curried Ono Cubes in Cataplana

SERVES 2–4

1 pound ono or other tuna, cut in
   cubes
1 tablespoon Yellow Pincho (page
   106) or curry seasoning
1/2 medium onion, chopped
2 tablespoons olive oil
1/4 cup dry white wine

When cooked, tuna tends to dry out. This is prevented by the enclosed environment of the cataplana, which is moist. Curries traveled from Goa to Macau to Portugal with the Portuguese. You can use a commercially blended curry powder or, as we did here, substitute Spanish Yellow Pincho seasoning, which is a close relative. Ono does not flake apart, so you end up with nice firm cubes. This recipe also works with swordfish or shark.

1 Toss the fish cubes with the Yellow Pincho and set aside.

2 In a medium cataplana, sweat the onion in the olive oil over a low heat until soft, about 20 minutes. Stir in the white wine, increasing the heat to bring ingredients to a boil. Add the fish and toss to coat. Close the cataplana and cook until the fish is done, approximately 10 minutes, gently shaking the cataplana occasionally to prevent sticking.

3 This can be served in a variety of ways, alone as an appetizer or with rice as an entree. To serve as a tapa, just stick a toothpick in each cube of fish, in which case, you should have about a dozen portions.

Chicken and Shiitake Mushrooms

SERVES 2

1/4 cup olive oil
1 choriço, diced
1 medium yellow onion, chopped
1 medium potato, diced
1 bay leaf
1/2 pound shiitake mushrooms, sliced
1/2 pound chicken breast, cut into strips
1/2 teaspoon sea salt
1/2 cup Madeira
1/2 cup half-and-half

In this case, you are using the enclosed environment of the cataplana to make a stew. That means you will have to be a little patient while it stews, hidden out of sight under its clamped-down lid. While it stews away, it is a good time to sip some of the Madeira—a good excuse to buy something a little better than Rainwater Madeira. A five-year-old Bual or a Malmsey would be a good selection (For more about Madeira, see A Dessert Wine Tasting, page 196).

1 Heat the oil in a large cataplana. Cook the choriço until it just starts to brown. Stir in the onion, potato, and bay leaf, and cook until the onion is limp. Add the mushrooms; stir and cook until softened. Stir in the chicken and salt. Pour in the Madeira, clamp down the cover, and cook 20 minutes. Open the cataplana and stir in the half-and-half just before serving.

Wine from Rueda

Classical Wines was one of the first importers of white wine from Rueda. Located along the Duero River in Castilla y León, Rueda is known for white wines made for the most part from the local Verdejo grape but also from Sauvignon Blanc. The wines have a hint of gold and hazelnuts. They pair perfectly with both poultry and mushroom flavors.

Azorean Beef Stew

SERVES 2

2 strips bacon, diced
1 pound beef steak, cubed
1/2 medium onion, chopped
2 cloves garlic, chopped
1 bay leaf
1 medium potato, diced into 1/2-
  inch cubes
1 carrot, cut into 1/8-inch slices
1/4 cup tawny port
1/4 cup Pimenta Moída (page 105)
1/4 cup cilantro, chopped

Victor Couto, a former manager of the Seattle store, and his parents are from the Azores. Every year his father makes Pimenta Moída and his mother uses it to make *carne asada*, which is essentially the Azorean version of the old standard, pot roast. Here, we used the Pimenta Moída in a beef dish made quickly in a cataplana.

1 In a medium cataplana, slowly heat the bacon to release the fat, then increase heat and brown. Add the beef, turn up the heat and brown 5 minutes. Add the onions, garlic, and bay leaf, then wilt, about 5 minutes. Add the potato, carrot, port, and Pimenta Moída, lightly stirring to combine. Close the cataplana and cook 20 minutes over medium heat.

2 Carefully open the cataplana, as the steam can scald. Remove the bay leaf and stir in the cilantro and test potatoes with a fork. Close the lid and let rest a few minutes. Serve with a little Pimenta Moída on the side.

Pesquera

Not that many years ago there was the strange contradiction: although Spain's most respected and expensive red wine, *Vega Sicilia*, came from Ribera del Duero, the region was otherwise unknown and the chief agricultural product was sugar beets, not grapes. Then in 1972, a salesman of sugar beet harvesting equipment, Alejandro Fernandez, began making a wine he named for the town of *Pesquera*. Robert Parker, America's best known wine critic, raved about it and the rest is history. Now the road following the river is lined with wineries and modern plantings of trellised vines march smartly up the slopes behind them. The wines, with their velvety black fruit and soft ripe berry aromas are often described as feminine in comparison to the masculinity of traditional barrel-aged Riojas.

The Spanish Yellow Mortar

The rhythmic thump of a pestle in a mortar echoing through the white-washed walls of a village was once the first notice of dinner being prepared. It is actually easy to make all these sauces in a mortar with a pestle and patience, but more and more cooks turn automatically to the food processor. The traditional Spanish mortar is ceramic with a yellow glaze and decorated with green splotches. They are made in a range of sizes. I recommend using one from time to time, just for the tactile experience of quietly crushing and blending with the strength in your own wrists, rather than using a noisy burst of electricity.

Recipes for the Spanish Yellow Mortar

Tomate Frito

1/4 cup olive oil
4 tomatoes, skinned, seeded, and
   roughly chopped
1/2 teaspoon Spanish sea salt
1/2 teaspoon sugar
Pepper, to taste

You can buy very good tomate frito in cans and jars, or if you have some ripe tomatoes with flavor, you can make your own. A paella pan is good for making tomato sauces because it is shallow and with all the surface area, the sauce cooks down quickly.

1 Heat the olive oil in an 11-inch paella pan and add the tomatoes, salt, sugar, and pepper. Cook 15 minutes. Purée with a mortar and pestle or in a blender, food processor, or food mill. If using a food mill, tomatoes do not need to be skinned prior to cooking. The resulting sauce will be richer if you don't.

USING TOMATE FRITO
This sauce is used to flavor soups, beans, lentils, and sausage dishes.

Sofrito

1 medium onion, chopped
1/2 cup olive oil
2 cloves garlic, chopped
1 red bell pepper, finely chopped
1 ripe tomato, cut in half, seeds
   shaken out and grated, skin
   discarded

Sofrito, the basis of much Spanish cooking, is a trip to the vegetable garden cooked down into a lumpy sauce. Sofritos use various combinations of onions, garlic, fresh peppers, and tomatoes.

1 Cook the onion in the olive oil until translucent. Add the garlic and cook until limp. Add the bell pepper and cook very slowly and patiently until reduced to almost a mush. Add the tomato and cook until liquid evaporates.

USING SOFRITO
A sofrito is the start of almost any soup, stew, or casserole. A Spanish recipe will usually assume the cook will make a sofrito. They start, for example, "Make a sofrito of onions and green pepper . . . "

Pimenta Moída (Portuguese Crushed Red Pepper Sauce)

1 pound red peppers, hot or mild, or a mix
1/8 cup coarse sea salt
1 tablespoon red wine vinegar
Extra virgin olive oil

Your trouble is going to be, step one, finding fresh Azorean peppers. But necessity being the mother of invention, you will do what I did: use whatever fresh red peppers you can find.

1 To prepare the peppers, wash them and remove their stems. If the peppers are spicy, you can reduce the heat of the sauce by removing the seeds, otherwise include them.

2 Grind the peppers with the salt using an old-fashioned hand-cranked grinder, a sleek, modern food processor, or even a trusty blender. Put the ground peppers in a medium saucepan and bring to a boil for 5 minutes. Stir in the vinegar and pour this mixture into a clean jar. When cool, cover the surface with a float of olive oil and refrigerate. This sauce reaches its peak after 3–4 months.

USING PIMENTA MOÍDA
In the Azores, this sauce is also rubbed into a whole, butterflied chicken before it is barbecued over hot coals.

I like to include ¼ cup Pimenta Moída rather than salt in the liquid when cooking fresh green beans.

Spanish Basting Oil

4 cloves garlic, chopped
1 teaspoon Spanish sea salt
1 pinch saffron threads
1 tablespoon bittersweet smoked pimentón
1/2 cup Spanish olive oil

I use this with chicken and pork.

1 Using a mortar and pestle, crush the garlic, salt, and saffron until they form a paste. Incorporate the pimentón, then the olive oil.

USING SPANISH BASTING OIL
When roasting or barbecuing, apply to meat, poultry, or fish with a pastry brush.

Pincho Seasoning

YELLOW PINCHO SEASONING

1 tablespoon salt
1 tablespoon turmeric
1 teaspoon garlic powder
1 bay leaf, ground
1 teaspoon pimentón dulce
1 teaspoon sugar
1/2 teaspoon coriander seed

RED PINCHO SEASONING
1 tablespoon salt
1 tablespoon pimentón agridulce
1 teaspoon sugar
1 teaspoon garlic powder
1/2 teaspoon thyme
1/2 teaspoon cumin
Black pepper, to taste

Like curry powder in the United States, pincho seasoning is a common spice blend sold premixed in Spain. If you want to try blending your own, here are the common ingredients in order of quantity used. As you will note, salt rules in Spain.

1 To blend, place ingredients in a food processor or spice mill and pulse until well blended.

USING PINCHO SEASONING
For the tapa bar standard, *patatas bravas*, roughly cut potatoes into 1-inch chunks and place in a cazuela. Toss with oil and red pincho seasoning. Cook in a hot oven or on a covered barbecue until easily pierced with a fork. Alioli is often served on top or alongside these spiced-up potatoes

Portuguese Basting Oil

4 cloves garlic, chopped
1 teaspoon coarse sea salt
1 bay leaf, crumbled
1/4 cup Piri Piri Sauce (facing page)
1/4 cup Portuguese olive oil

The Portuguese embrace *picante*, spicy-hot. Piri Piri puts some heat in this oil.

1 Using a mortar and pestle, crush the garlic, salt, and bay leaf, then work in the Piri Piri Sauce and the oil. Thoroughly combine.

USING PORTUGUESE BASTING OIL
Using a pastry brush, I completely cover a chicken with this mixture prior to roasting and reapply several times as it cooks.

Pisto

1 onion, chopped
2 cloves garlic, finely chopped
1/2 cup olive oil
1 eggplant, roughly chopped
2 bell peppers, one green and one
  red or yellow, roughly chopped
2 tomatoes, very ripe, roughly
  chopped
1 zucchini, roughly chopped
1/4 teaspoon Pebrella (or oregano,
  or thyme and/or cumin)
1 tablespoon minced parsley
Pinch salt
1 tablespoon red wine vinegar
Splash extra virgin olive oil

This is not actually a sauce, but then perhaps it is. It differs from sofrito in that it includes additional vegetables such as eggplant and zucchini. It differs from *Escalivada* (page 168) in that the vegetables are cubed rather than sliced lengthwise, so the result is chunky, and then it is cooked down to a marmalade consistency. In *cocina pobre*, it is served topped with a fried egg. The Catalans claim they taught this dish to the Provençal French, who call it *ratatouille*. It actually is much more likely to be Arabic in origin.

1 Cook the onions and garlic slowly and patiently in the olive oil. Add the eggplant and the bell pepper and cook until soft. Add the tomatoes and cook until the liquid evaporates. Then add the zucchini and cook until soft. Season with herbs and add the parsley. Salt to taste and correct the acidity with some vinegar if needed. This will depend on the vegetables. Now add a splash of extra virgin olive oil.

USING PISTO
Pisto can be served hot or at room temperature as a side dish. Or try cooking a chicken in this sauce. Or toss it with some pasta. If it is used on baked white fish, you have a delicious result, something akin to the Mexican preparation for fish a la Veracruz. Pisto is also used as a topping for coca, Catalan pizza.

Piri Piri Sauce

1 jar (2.25 ounces) whole piri
  piri peppers packed in vinegar,
  divided
1 tablespoon extra course sea salt
1 bay leaf
1 tablespoon brandy
1 cup dry white wine

Every chef has his own formula for Piri Piri Sauce, starting with the peppers and salt, and then adding vinegar, olive oil, brandy, and perhaps garlic or bay leaf or lemon peels. It is often kept in a bottle next to the grill.

1 Drain the peppers, reserving the brine and three of the peppers.

2 Put the salt in a mortar with the remaining peppers and thoroughly mash them. When reduced to a paste, stir in the reserved brine.

3 Place the three whole peppers and the bay leaf in a clean 375 milliliter wine bottle. Add the paste and top off with brandy and white wine.

USING PIRI PIRI SAUCE
Baste prawns or steak before grilling.

Picada

1/2 cup almonds and/or hazelnuts
and/or pine nuts
1 tablespoon olive oil
1/2 cup stale bread cubes
1/4 teaspoon coarse Spanish sea
salt
1 clove garlic, roughly chopped
1 tablespoon minced parsley
2 tablespoons extra virgin olive oil

Spanish bread goes stale quickly, so Spanish cooks have many ways to make use of leftover pieces of loaves, from Gazpacho to Migas. Both Picada and Romesco use a combination of stale bread and powdered nuts to make a thick paste.

1 Brown the nuts in oil. Remove and let cool. Add the bread to the oil and brown.

2 Place the nuts and salt in a mortar and crush with a pestle or use a food processor and pulse to chop nuts. If using an electrical appliance, be careful not to turn them into nut butter.

3 Add the garlic and parsley and blend until mixed. Add the bread cubes and pulse until it reaches the texture of bread crumbs. Drizzle in the olive oil and combine.

USING PICADA
Picada is typically used to thicken a sauce or stew. It is usually added at the end, shortly before the dish is served to add substance and subtle complexity to the sauce.

Wine from Rioja

The white grape of Rioja is the under-appreciated Viura (Macabeo in Catalonia). Two approaches are used to make wines from it. One, the modern style, uses stainless steel, temperature controlled fermentation to make light bodied, dry wines that are brightly flavored with a lively acidity that complements the light foods usually paired with white wines such as poultry and fish. The other style amplifies the wine with oak, either through barrel fermentation or aging in cask. These are perfect for people fond of oaken Chardonnay.

Romesco

4 to 5 ñora peppers, rehydrated with boiling water (if not available, use 4 tablespoons sweet pimentón)

1/4 cup almonds (preferably Marcona) and/or hazelnuts and/or pine nuts (in a pinch, walnuts can even be used)

2 tablespoons olive oil

1 slice (1/2 cup) stale bread, cubed

1 clove garlic, roughly chopped

1 teaspoon coarse sea salt

1 small hot red guindilla pepper (cayena pepper), optional

1 tomato, optional, peeled and seeded (roasting the tomato adds depth)

1 sprig parsley, optional

1 tablespoon red wine vinegar or sherry vinegar, optional

4 tablespoons reserved liquid from ñoras

2 tablespoons extra virgin olive oil, if needed

Romesco is a Catalan sauce of red ñora peppers, garlic, vinegar, and hazelnuts or almonds with stale bread as a thickener. It is one of those sauces of infinite variation with every cook having different proportions and variations on the ingredients.

1 Cover ñoras with water and bring to a boil. Allow to steep half an hour. Remove stems and seeds, saving flesh and skin, reserving the liquid.

2 Sauté nuts in oil until brown; remove with a slotted spoon. Sauté the bread in the oil, adding more oil if needed.

3 Place the garlic and salt in a mortar and blend together with a pestle or put them in a food processor and give it a couple of bursts. If making a spicy version, add the hot pepper.

4 Add the cooled nuts to the bread and grind. Add the ñora and the reserved liquid, and blend in. If using tomato, blend it in now. If using parsley, add it now. Season with a splash of vinegar. If serving with vegetables, go a little heavier on the vinegar. If using with fish,

use a lighter hand or omit. If the sauce is too thick, add a splash of extra virgin olive oil.

5 As with all sauces, running this sauce through a food mill makes a smoother, more sophisticated product. Leave it chunky for cocina pobre.

USING ROMESCO
Romesco is served in the spring in Catalonia with calçots, onion shoots, charred over an open fire. Use your imagination with this salsa, pairing it with grilled fresh green asparagus, grilled green onion, or even cooked beets.

The sauce's rich flavor also goes wonderfully with seafood such as prawns or salmon. Grill salmon, then brush the top with a thick coating of Romesco. For a dipping sauce for fried calamari, combine 1/3 cup Romesco with 2/3 cup Alioli.

Extra Virgin Olive Oil Mayonesa

1 egg yolk or whole egg
2 tablespoons lemon juice
1/2 teaspoon salt
Pinch mustard
1 cup extra virgin olive oil

Mayonesa (mahonesa) was probably named after Mahón, the port city of Menorca, one of the Balearic Islands off Catalonia in the Mediterranean. The Catalans claim they invented it but, of course, so do the French.

1 Blend all ingredients except olive oil with a mortar and pestle or in a food processor and then add the olive oil very slowly (many food possessors have a hole in the cover of the feed tube designed to trickle liquids into the bowl while the motor is running) until the desired consistency.

2 I must admit that I was raised on commercial mayonnaise and have never been weaned off it. I make commercial mayonnaise taste Spanish by blending in a little strong-flavored Spanish extra virgin olive oil, such as one made from picual olives.

Olivada

1 cup pitted black olives
2 tablespoons extra virgin olive oil
Pinch coarse sea salt

This simple purée of black olive meat captures the richness of tree-ripened black olives. If time is short, it is faster to buy this in a jar and spare yourself the trouble of pitting each olive. It comes in several versions using empeltre or arbequina olives and even green olives, from both Spain and Portugal. But here are the ingredients if you are in a do-it-yourself mood.

1 Crush all ingredients together with a mortar and pestle or put in food processor and pulse gently until blended. It should have a coarse texture.

VARIATION To make olivada into a classic tapenade, add capers and anchovies.

USING OLIVADA
Spread the paste on bread, bread fried in olive oil, or crackers, and serve it just that way. For color and flavor contrast, garnish with a parsley leaf, or sprinkle a little crushed oregano over it, or top off with half of a pitted green olive. A slice of hard-boiled egg or an artichoke heart quarter adds a layer of interest.

Blend 1/2 cup olivada with a room temperature stick of butter for a creamy spread for fresh bread.

Or cook some fresh green beans, drain, and toss them with this paste while still hot, with or without adding some finely chopped garlic, raw or softened in olive oil. Elaborate this further by tossing the beans dressed in Olivada with pasta.

Alioli

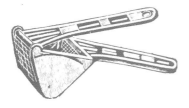

In Catalonia this garlic version of mayonnaise is made from olive oil and purple-skinned garlic but without eggs. Elsewhere in Spain eggs are included. Alioli adds healthy, rich flavor wherever you might have been tempted to use a dab of mayonnaise.

1 A quick way to make garlic mayonnaise is to mash up some chopped garlic, adding a little Spanish extra virgin olive oil until a rich paste is formed, then stir in commercial mayonnaise. How much garlic you use is a judgment call.

2 A little bread can be added when making alioli or mashing a little cooked potato into the garlic before adding the oil is another variation. If you mix some shredded white fish with garlic mashed potatoes, you have the classic Spanish spread, brandad, which can also be used as a stuffing for piquillo peppers.

USING ALIOLI
• For a hot tapa, turn mushroom caps upside down, spoon a little alioli into the cup and broil them.
• You can add Alioli to mashed potatoes for garlic mashed potatoes.
• After you have removed chops or steaks from the grill, top them off with a tablespoon of Alioli.

FLAVORING MAYONESA OR ALIOLI
To add an interesting extra burst, you can flavor either Extra Virgin Olive Oil Mayonesa or Alioli by blending in spices or small amounts of sauces. Here are some things to crush in a mortar and mix in.

Saffron
Capers
Anchovies
Pimentón
Romesco

These can be used as dipping sauces or used when constructing *montaditos*.

White Sauce

2 tablespoons butter
2 tablespoons flour
1 cup whole milk
¼ teaspoon salt

This is a very basic recipe. For a sauce with authentic Andalucian aroma and flavor, add a healthy splash of sherry (about 2 tablespoons). For most recipes, I prefer the nutty taste of an Amontillado sherry, but for this, use whatever you have on hand. For a touch of Portugal, add a splash of Madeira or tawny port. If seeking the more rustic flavor of cocina pobre, make the white sauce using olive oil rather than the traditional butter.

1 Melt the butter in a saucepan and then whisk in the flour. Slowly add the milk, stirring continuously, until it thickens and is heated. Add salt to taste.

PINK-WHITE SAUCE VARIATION
White sauce is used in this cookbook in conjunction with piquillo peppers, so the natural juice in which they are packed should be added to the white sauce as well as a purée of the least attractive pepper in the container. Another alternative is to add ½ to 1 teaspoon pimentón.

GREEN-WHITE SAUCE VARIATION
Purée roasted green pepper and incorporate it into the sauce.

Saffron Syrup

1 cup sugar
1 cup water
Pinch saffron

A simple sugar syrup flavored with saffron quickly lends the flavor of Spain to many dishes.

1 Stir the sugar and water together in a medium saucepan, bringing to a gentle boil. Reduce heat and simmer 10 minutes. The bubbles should just break the surface. Remove from heat. Using a small mortar, grind the saffron to a powder. Add to the syrup, stirring until evenly distributed and the syrup takes on a lovely orange hue.

USING SAFFRON SYRUP
• Sweeten freshly brewed jasmine or mint tea. A drop is good. It is great in ice tea served with slice of lemon.
• Replace the sugar in sweet breads with saffron syrup.
• Drizzle syrup over freshly baked sweet breads while still hot to create a glaze.
• Use the syrup to sweeten *arroz con leche*, *flan*, or *natillas*.
• Use it in place of sugar when sweetening whipping cream.

Saffron Candied Citrus Zest

Citrus fruit for zest
Saffron syrup
Water
Sugar (optional)

It is easy to candy citrus zest with saffron syrup. Using a zester or vegetable peeler, cut the colored part of the peel off a lemon, orange, or grapefruit leaving the white portion of the peel on the fruit. If using a vegetable peeler, you can julienne the slabs of skin if you want thin strips. The broader slabs can be left intact, candied, and sugared and served as a treat in and of themselves or diced and added to breads when baking.

1 Put zest in a small saucepan, just coat with saffron syrup and add water to cover. Simmer over low heat until zest is translucent. This should take less than 10 minutes. Remove from heat and allow to steep as they cool. Store in syrup, or using a mesh strainer, drain and allow to air dry.

2 Alternatively, zest can be rolled in sugar to coat.

USING CANDIED CITRUS ZEST
Candied citrus zest strips can be used as a garnish when serving a dessert or as a decoration on cakes and tarts. It can also be added as a dice to add a sweet and sour element to sauces.

CITRUS SLICES VARIATION
Whole slices of citrus fruit can be candied in the same way. Use a medium saucepan. It will take up to 45 minutes for slices to become translucent. When done, dry the slices on a wire rack or coat with sugar. Slices can be stored buried in sugar in the refrigerator until needed.

Saffron Candied Nuts

1/2 cup Marcona almonds, pine nuts, or walnuts
2 tablespoons saffron syrup

The Spanish harvest includes a wealth of nuts. Candied, they are a special treat.

1 Place nuts and syrup in a medium saucepan and cook over medium heat approximately 5 minutes until syrup begins to brown. Remove to plate to cool. The nuts may be a little sticky while hot, but the coating should harden as they cool. If they start to stick together, break apart.

USING SAFFRON CANDIED NUTS
Serve as a tapa, in salads, with desserts, whole, or chopped.

COCINA POBRE

Poor Food

Cocina Pobre, poor food, is meals born of poverty and shaped by frugality. Throughout history, Spain has long had pockets of rural poverty and lower classes living in urban areas on meager means. Every scrap and every crust of stale bread was used for food. Sometimes, meals were fashioned out of almost nothing. In *I'll Dress You in Mourning*, the bull fighter El Cordobés recalls growing up during those lean years in Andalucía when he ate meals of grass soup. Necessity is the mother of invention.

Recipes for Cocina Pobre

Dusty Olives

SERVES 3

1 cup mixed olives, green, black, and arbequina
1 teaspoon pimentón
1 teaspoon sherry vinegar
2 tablespoons extra virgin olive oil
1/2 cup piquillo strips, optional

This is a quick and easy tapa.

1 Toss the olives with the pimentón and dress with the sherry vinegar and olive oil. Allow to marinate at least one hour. Add piquillo strips just before serving.

Marinated Olives

1/4 cup Spanish red wine or sherry vinegar
4 cloves garlic, crushed
2 lemon slices
1 teaspoon coriander seeds
2 teaspoons pebrella or thyme
1 sprig rosemary
1 bay leaf
1 dried, small, red guindilla chile (optional)
1 jar (14 ounces) olives

This is another tasty tapa.

1 Combine all of the ingredients except olives to create the marinade.

2 Drain the jar of olives and replace the liquid with this marinade. Store in the refrigerator. Fill any space left in the jar with water, or white or fino sherry.

Pimentón Bread Crumbs

Garlic crushed with the flat side of a knife
Olive oil
Pimentón
Bread crumbs

These flavorful bread crumbs can be sprinkled over a dish just before it is served. Instantly, you will have improved upon what you are serving by adding depth and complexity of flavor. A second sprinkling of minced parsley will add a touch of freshness. ☽ In the following recipe the proportions are, as the lawyers would note, deliberately left blank.

1 Cook the garlic in oil over medium heat until golden brown and then discard. Add the pimentón and cook for a minute. Add the bread crumbs, turning up the heat to toast them, stirring constantly. Use your nose to tell you when they are done.

Paula Wolfert's Pebrella-and-Membrillo-Marinated Olives

SERVES 6

2 cups gordal olives, green and black.
²/₃ ounce Spanish membrillo (quince paste)
¹/₂ teaspoon pebrella
1 lemon, roughly chopped, peel and all
¹/₄ cup extra virgin olive oil
1¹/₂ cups water, enough to cover the olives

Paula Wolfert asked me about pebrella one time in a telephone conversation. She had been introduced to it in Valencia where it is native. She had instructions from a bar in Alicante for marinating green olives in pebrella and membrillo but had never been able to put it in a cookbook because no one sold pebrella in the United States. I talked to our supplier of herbs in Novelda and after their initial shock that anyone in the United States had heard of pebrella, arranged for us to get some in our next shipment. It is in the thyme family and indigenous to a small area around Valencia and Alicante. Endangered in the wild, it is now grown commercially. Using the big green gordal olives makes a striking presentation. I often also add some black olives for color contrast but any olives work in a pinch.

1 Crush olives lightly with a meat tenderizer or kitchen mallet and place in a crock or jar. Combine marinating ingredients and pour over cracked olives. Marinate for two days or longer before serving as a tapa.

Bread and Tomato

A piece of bread
¹/₂ clove garlic
¹/₂ ripe tomato
Extra virgin olive oil
Salt

This seems simple. It is. It is just tomato-garlic bread. But it is as basic to the Catalan culinary culture as peanut butter and jam is to America.

1 Simply take a piece of bread or roll, usually toasted, usually a baguette split lengthwise, rub with half a raw garlic clove, then rub with half a ripe red tomato to extract its juices, then drizzle with extra virgin olive oil, and dust with salt.

VARIATION
To make it fancy, top it off by adding a thin sheet of jamón. Or, for fisherman's style, lay a couple of fillets of anchovy across the top.

Migas (Bread Crumbs)

Migas is another rustic Iberian dish using stale bread. It is the food of peasants, fashioned from what is left as the larder becomes threadbare.

SERVES 2

1/4 cup Spanish olive oil
2 cloves garlic, minced
1/2 cup jamón trimmings, the fattier the better, diced
1/2 cup chorizo, diced
1 onion, chopped
1 tablespoon bittersweet pimentón
4 cups cubed stale bread
1 cup chicken stock or water, divided

1 Preheat oven to 350 degrees F.

2 Heat the oil in a 10-inch cazuela and sauté garlic until just golden. Add the jamón and cook until fat is rendered. Add the chorizo. When the chorizo is sizzling hot, add the onion and cook until translucent. Stir in the pimentón and cook for a minute, and then add the bread and toss. Add 1/2 cup chicken stock and toss. Sprinkle the remaining 1/2 cup of stock over the bread and cover (if using a regular cazuela without a top, cover with foil).

3 Bake 10 minutes. Remove foil and bake an additional 10 minutes.

4 This is a fairly uptown version using chicken stock. Tap water works fine. In Spain this is a dish made of leftovers and scraps so don't worry too much about the measurements or ingredients— experiment. If migas are stuffed into a sausage casing, it is *farinato*.

Sephardic Migas

SERVES 2

1/4 cup Portuguese olive oil
1 onion, chopped
2 cloves garlic, minced
1 cup poultry scraps (chicken, turkey, or whatever you have), chopped
1 tablespoon bittersweet pimentón
4 cups cubed stale bread
1 cup chicken stock

The origination of this sausage is dated to 1492 and the commencement of the overt persecution of the Jews. The eating of pig, even the butchering of pigs, was a symbol of Catholicity. The idea was to make these sausages so that a Jew could appear to be eating pork. The result has survived because it was delicious. Because you probably do not have casings with which to make your own link sausage, here is a version of migas without pork.

1 Preheat oven to 350 degrees F.

2 Heat the oil in a 10-inch cazuela with a top. Sauté the onion and garlic until soft. Add the poultry scraps and cook through. Stir in the pimentón and then add the bread and chicken stock and cover (if using a regular cazuela without a top, cover with foil).

3 Bake 10 minutes. Remove foil and bake an additional 10 minutes. Serve as a side dish right in the cazuela.

Amy's Chorizo Bread Pudding

SERVES 4

3 eggs
2 cups cream (you can use half milk)
1 loaf crusty bread, cut into cubes
2 tablespoons butter
1 medium yellow onion, diced
1/4 pound semi-cured chorizo, diced
1/2 teaspoon salt
1/4 teaspoon pepper

At their Seattle restaurant Eva, The Spanish Table's former wine manager, James Hondros, and his wife, Amy, do a version of migas elevating it to Chorizo Bread Pudding by adding eggs, butter, and cream, which they serve with Amontillado Sherry Braised Rabbit.

1 Preheat oven to 350 degrees F. Butter a large casserole dish.

2 Whisk together the eggs and cream. Add the bread and toss to coat.

3 In a sauté pan, melt the butter over medium heat, and then sauté the onion, but do not brown. When the onion softens, add the chorizo and toss. Stir the onions and chorizo into the bread and cream mixture. Add salt and pepper. Pour into the prepared casserole and bake until custard is set and the top is slightly brown, approximately 35–45 minutes.

Açorda (Portuguese Bread Soup)

SERVES 6

1/4 cup olive oil
3 cups cubed stale bread
12 to 18 prawns, depending on size
6 cloves garlic, chopped
1 bay leaf, crushed
1 tablespoon bittersweet smoked
  pimentón
1 teaspoon coarse sea salt
1/4 cup extra virgin olive oil
6 cups fish stock or clam juice
Dash Piri Piri Sauce (page 107)
1/4 cup minced cilantro
2 eggs

This is one of those concoctions born of poverty, using up a few pieces of stale bread in frugal circumstances that soars above its humble origin.

1 Place oil in a large olla and heat until a haze forms. Fry the bread until golden, and then remove with slotted spoon. Add the prawns and cook lightly. In a mortar, mash the garlic, bay leaf, pimentón, and sea salt to a paste, adding the extra virgin olive oil. Stir into the ingredients in the olla. Add the stock and Piri Piri Sauce. Add the fried bread and cilantro. Bring to a rolling boil, remove from heat, and then break the eggs and float on the surface and cover. The açorda is presented immediately at the table, the cover removed and the eggs stirred in with the ladle. The aromas that emerge as it is served are exquisite.

Garlic and Bread Soup

SERVES 6

6 cloves garlic, unpeeled, crushed
  with the side of a knife
4 tablespoons olive oil
3 cups cubed stale bread
1 tablespoon bittersweet smoked
  pimentón
1 teaspoon coarse sea salt
2 tablespoons extra virgin olive oil
6 cups chicken broth
1 bay leaf
1 ñora pepper, stem removed
1 cup Tomate Frito (page 104),
  optional
Dash Piri Piri Sauce (page 107),
  optional
3 tablespoons minced parsley or
  cilantro
6 eggs, optional

One night in Cuenca, the restaurant Figón de Pedro served us a soup made with bread, garlic, onion, and asparagus tips. That was a very fancy elaboration of the peasant soup that is, at its most elemental, garlic boiled in water and poured over stale bread. My version uses chicken broth, that elaborates for a rich stock. You have a lot of options. One is adding cilantro and Piri Piri Sauce to give the soup a little *beijinho* from Portugal.

1 Sauté the garlic cloves in the olive oil until golden, and then remove with a slotted spoon.

2 Using the same oil, fry the bread until golden.

3 In a mortar, mash the garlic, pimentón, and salt to a paste, adding the extra virgin olive oil. Place the paste in an olla with the broth, bay leaf, ñora pepper, and optional Tomate Frito and/or Piri Piri Sauce and bring to a rolling boil. Reduce heat and simmer until flavors are infused throughout the broth.

4 Divide the fried bread between six soup bowls and sprinkle with parsley or cilantro. Return broth to a boil, and one at a time, ladle boiling liquid over the bread and quickly break an egg into each bowl so it poaches. If you want a lighter version, omit the eggs or add a single egg to the pot and stir it in before ladling the soup into the bowls.

Açorda Pudim (Bread Pudding)

This is the simple dish elaborated. The açorda is transformed into a bread pudding, molded, and served with prawns whose flavor infuses the bread pudding.

SERVES 6

18 to 24 large prawns
Pinch sea salt
6 black peppercorns
1 bay leaf
Water
2 tablespoons minced garlic
2 tablespoons olive oil
3 cups bread, diced
2 tablespoons minced cilantro
2 eggs
1/2 cup half-and-half

1 Preheat oven to 350 degrees F. Place the prawns, salt, peppercorns, and bay leaf in a covered saucepan with water to cover. Bring to a boil and cook until the prawns are opaque.

2 Allow to cool, reserving the cooking liquid. Peel the prawns and return shells to water. Boil uncovered until liquid is reduced to about 1/2 cup. Strain the liquid and reserve.

3 Soften the garlic in olive oil and then toss with the bread. Add the cilantro and toss.

4 Beat eggs into the reserved cooking liquid with the half-and-half, adding salt to taste.

5 Mix with bread. For individual servings, bake in a nonstick or well-oiled muffin tin until firm and tops begin to brown, approximately 20–30 minutes. You can also bake in a 10-inch quiche pan approximately 20–30 minutes. Serve with the boiled prawns.

Fisherman's Pot

This is a dish fishermen make out of the leftovers from their nights out on a wine-dark sea setting and pulling nets from a hand-oared dory—those brightly painted, sturdy wooden boats named after saints and wives that photographers love so much. It is nothing but the little fish left over after the restaurants and housewives have picked over their catch, plus a couple of potatoes and an onion. If you want it to taste to you the way it does to the fisherman, you need to drink a glass of brandy as an aperitif.

SERVES 2 FISHERMEN, 4 LESS HEARTY EATERS

Olive oil
3 medium potatoes, thinly sliced, divided
1 large onion, thinly sliced, divided
1 pound small fish fillets, Dover sole or mixed species, divided (Preferably the smallest and least expensive available. Bottom fish are great.)
Pinch Spanish sea salt
Pinch freshly ground black pepper
1/2 cup Spanish extra virgin olive oil
1 tablespoon chopped parsley

1 Preheat oven to 350 degrees F.

2 Oil the bottom of an 8-inch cazuela. Cover the bottom with the slices of one of the potatoes, overlapping them like roof tiles. Add a layer of 1/3 of the onion, and then a layer of 1/3 of the fish. Dust with salt and pepper. Repeat twice until you have three layers. Pour the olive oil over the stack like pouring syrup over a stack of hot cakes. Sprinkle with the parsley.

3 Bake 50 minutes while sipping your brandy.

Patatas à la Riojana (Rustic Potatoes)

SERVES 4

1 onion, cut into eight wedges
1/4 cup olive oil
4 Spanish-style cooking chorizo, cut into 3/8-inch-thick slices
1 tablespoon bittersweet pimentón, or 1 dried choricero pepper, reconstituted
1 bay leaf
1 teaspoon Spanish sea salt
3 pounds potatoes, cut into chunks
Water to cover

This very traditional rustic dish can be served as a soup course. The term *a la riojana* refers to the inclusion of dried peppers (in this case, use pimentón unless you have access to a whole dried choricero pepper).

1 Sauté the onion in olive oil until limp. Add the chorizo and cook until the fat is released.

2 Stir in pimentón, then add the bay leaf, salt, and potatoes, and cover with water and bring to a boil. Simmer until potatoes are soft. Serve in individual bowls.

Serve with a Rioja

This is a great dish to serve with a Rioja wine that has seen some oak, such as a Crianza, or if you prefer a white, a barrel-fermented Rioja blanco. White wine from Rioja has come into its own over the past fifteen years and now surprises people with its freshness and high quality at a low, low price.

Boiled Potatoes and Onions

SERVES 4

1 pound potatoes, cut into chunks
1 large onion, cut into wedges
1 pound green beans, cut into 1-inch lengths
Water to cover
1 teaspoon coarse Spanish sea salt, plus an additional pinch, divided
1/2 cup Spanish extra virgin olive oil

A dish of zen-like simplicity, the vegetables' flavors meld and complement each other, an example of a sum that is greater than its parts.

1 Place the three vegetables in an olla large enough to hold them. Cover with water, add salt, and boil until the potatoes can be pierced with a fork. Drain (the cooking water, if saved, is a good stock for making soups). Drizzle with olive oil and sprinkle with salt before serving.

Garlic Mashed Potatoes with Broccoli Florets

SERVES 6

Water
1 tablespoon salt
1 pound broccoli
6 pounds potatoes, peeled and cut into quarters
1/2 cup butter
4 cloves garlic

This Portuguese dish works well as a side to your meat of choice.

1 Fill a large saucepan with water and bring to a boil. Add the salt. Cook the broccoli until just tender and remove and let cool.

2 Place the potatoes in the water and cook until easily pierced with a fork and then drain, reserving a little of the cooking liquid.

3 In the same pan, melt the butter and sauté the garlic until soft. Return the potatoes to the pan and mash together with the butter and garlic, adding reserved cooking liquid to thin if necessary. Break the broccoli up into florets and chop up the tender stems. Mix the broccoli into the potatoes and serve.

Iberian Villages by Raymond F. Carver, Jr.

One of the questions I am most frequently asked is how I happened to fall in love with Spain. This book has to be included in the answer. On seven trips to Spain in the 1970s, architect Raymond F. Carver, Jr. photographed the historic villages of Spain and Portugal from the medieval stone structures of the north to the whitewashed hill towns of the south. In 1981, he selected 186 black and white photographs for his book, Iberian Villages, Portugal and Spain. The strength of these reverent images lured us out onto the back roads of Spain, the real home of cocina pobre.

ENTERTAINING

Celebrating With Friends

Spain and Portugal are family oriented societies, and their food always blends in perfectly at group gatherings from family reunions to formal dinner parties to comfort food for two. Their cuisine can be as elegant as what is served in a trendy restaurant, or as rustic as the fare in a country bar, but it is always flavorful and appetizing.

I have suggested nine occasions to celebrate Spanish and Portuguese style. And since special parties and gatherings are always enhanced by music, I have shared a few of my ideas and opinions by matching up the events with music.

Recipes for Entertaining

Valentine's Day Dinner

This is one night that, if you are warm-blooded, you are destined to feel at least a little more romantic than usual. Maybe this menu will inspire a memorable evening. When all the dishes are ready, pause to slip into your most alluring evening wear, be it a dress or tuxedo, and reappear for a glass of cava by candlelight.

Valentine's Day Music
Portuguese Fado

Fado is a music of late nights. It is sung in the cellar bars on the cobblestone alleys just off the docks of Lisbon. With its coves and harbors opening out onto the Atlantic, Portugal is a nation of sailors. Sailors leave broken hearts.

The sad faces of mothers and the lonely faces of lovers have long stared out to sea. Fado, music born of this sadness, is filled with melancholy and longing. The songs are meant to carry out to sea, to bring a darling one home from their voyage, back to the arms of their families and lovers.

The late Amália Rodrigues was the diva of fado and remains so today, but there is a renewed interest in fado and young stars are leading its revival: Mariza, Misía, Mafalda Arnauth, and many others. These young voices, reinterpreting the music and lyrics, make the past, present, and the future seem inseparable.

Mussels Steamed in Cava in a Cataplana

SERVES 2

1 tablespoon olive oil
1/4 cup minced chives
12 green peppercorns packed in brine, rinsed, and crushed with a pestle
1/4 teaspoon grated lemon zest
1/4 cup cava
1/8 pound baby shrimp meat
1/2 pound mussels, washed and de-bearded

Seafood and sparkling wines not only belong together, but they are said, by people who should know, to have the components of an aphrodisiac. Therefore we suggest drinking the cava remaining in the bottle as this dish cooks. The recipe does not include garlic for obvious reasons. The decadent touch of the addition of shrimp meat adds complexity and color.

1 Heat the oil in a medium cataplana and stir in the chives, peppercorns, zest, and cava, and heat just to a boil. Add the shrimp and mussels and clamp the lid of cataplana closed. Cook 5 minutes, or until all the mussels are open.

CAVA

Why is it called cava? Prior to the European Union, Spain used the word champaña, or in Catalan, xampana, for sparkling wine. However, now words similar to champagne can only be used by the French. The Spanish have adopted the word *cava*, cave, for their sparkling wines. The change in terminology has turned out well, because the grapes used in cava are unique to Spain, and therefore its sparkling wines are unique and distinctive.

White Asparagus Spears with Piquillo Pepper Dressing

SERVES 2

2 piquillo peppers, cut into strips
1 jar white asparagus spears, drained

THE DRESSING
1 piquillo pepper
1/4 cup extra virgin olive oil
1 1/2 tablespoons sherry vinegar
1/2 teaspoon minced parsley
1 teaspoon sweet pimentón
Pinch salt
Grind black pepper
1/8 teaspoon sugar
1/8 teaspoon Dijon mustard
1/8 teaspoon pebrella

Spears of white asparagus and piquillo peppers from Navarra are Spanish staples. The piquillo-pimentón sauce adds color and complexity. It is a simple salad, one that uses preserved vegetables as is appropriate in the dead of winter.

1 Divide the asparagus onto individual serving plates and place piquillo strips artfully across them. Drizzle with dressing.

2 To make the dressing, place piquillo pepper in a blender with the other ingredients and purée until smooth. There will be dressing left over.

Piquillo Peppers Stuffed with Dungeness Crab

SERVES 2 OR TAPAS FOR 6

2 tablespoons Amontillado or cream sherry
$1/2$ cup White Sauce (page 112), divided
$1/4$ pound Dungeness crabmeat
$1/2$ cup dry white wine
1 tablespoon Picada (page 108)
1 tablespoon minced parsley, divided
6 piquillo peppers

The sweet tanginess of piquillo peppers enhances the richness of the Dungeness crab. The sherry adds sinfully Spanish aromas. The peppers are red as hearts pulsing love.

1 Preheat oven to 350 degrees F.

FILLING

2 Whisk sherry into $1/4$ cup of the White Sauce and heat until fully incorporated. Remove from the heat and fold in the crab. Let cool while you make the sauce.

SAUCE

3 Combine the remaining White Sauce with the white wine. Heat and then whisk in the Picada and half the parsley.

4 Holding the piquillo peppers suspended between your thumb and forefinger, spoon the crab mixture into them. Place the peppers in a 10-inch cazuela, with the points toward the center so they form a rose.

5 Spoon the sauce over the stuffed peppers and bake until they are hot in the center, about 20 minutes. Sprinkle the remaining parsley across the top.

Pebrella-Scented Game Hen

SERVES 2

1 Rock Cornish game hen
2 teaspoons pebrella
$1/2$ teaspoon coarse sea salt
1 tablespoon minced parsley
2 tablespoons olive oil
$1/2$ 1emon, juiced
$1^{1}/2$ cups chicken stock
$1/2$ cup Argentine polenta (Argentine polenta cooks in a minute, is bright yellow, and tastes of corn. If not available, cook polenta according to the instructions on the package)
$1/2$ cup chopped cilantro
$1/4$ cup grated Manchego cheese
1 tablespoon extra virgin olive oil

These little birds are delicious messengers of love.

1 Preheat oven to 400 degrees F. Cut the game hen open with a pair of poultry shears and butterfly.

2 Place the pebrella and salt in a mortar and crush them together with a pestle. Add the parsley and grind that into the mix. Incorporate the olive oil slowly, forming a thick paste. Work in the lemon juice.

3 Put the game hen in a large cazuela and brush it on both sides with this mix.

4 Bake the game hen for 30 minutes and check to ensure it is done. If so, remove the bird from the cazuela.

5 On the stovetop, deglaze the pan with the chicken stock. Add the polenta. Bring the polenta to a boil, stirring constantly. It will thicken instantly. Stir in the cilantro and the cheese. Turn off the heat and stir in the extra virgin olive oil. Place the bird on top of the polenta and serve.

Chocolate Torta Valenciana

SERVES 8

¼ cup blanched Marcona almonds
2 tablespoons pine nuts
5½ ounces bittersweet chocolate, chopped
3 teaspoons minced orange zest
6 large eggs, separated, at room temperature
½ cup sugar, divided
Whipped cream
Saffron Candied Citrus Zest (page 113)

My wife, Sharon, falls into the category of dessert eaters generally referred to as chocoholics, while I prefer fruit and nut flavors. This dessert satisfies us both because the richness of the chocolate in this cake is balanced by the flavor of oranges, almonds, and pine nuts. Whipping the separated eggs incorporates enough air into the batter to lend it an unexpected lightness.

1 Preheat oven to 350 degrees F. Toast the nuts in a sauté pan until golden in color. Then place in a food processor with the chocolate and orange zest and pulse until they form a paste.

2 Whip the egg yolks and ¼ cup of the sugar with an electric mixer on high for 3 minutes until slightly increased in volume. Reduce the mixer speed to low and incorporate the chocolate mixture, forming a stiff batter.

3 Wash the beaters and whip the egg whites with the remaining sugar until they form stiff peaks. Gently fold half of the egg whites into the chocolate-egg yolk batter, then the other half, gently mixing until incorporated.

4 Gently ease the batter into a 9-inch cake pan lined with parchment paper. Bake 25 minutes, or until a cake tester inserted in center comes out clean.

5 Remove the cake from the pan and cool before topping with whipped cream and a sprinkle of Saffron Candied Citrus Zest.

Chocolate Cake with Saffron-Scented Whipped Cream

1 prebaked or store-bought chocolate cake
1 cup heavy cream (not "whipping cream" which is presweetened)
3 tablespoons Saffron Syrup (page 112)

So perhaps you do not have time to make chocolate cake when preparing an elegant dinner for two? Here is a way to put Spanish make-up on a store-bought dessert. For a golden yellow, florally fragrant topping, we use saffron syrup to replace sugar in whipped cream.

1 With the mixer blurring at high speed and the heavy cream nearly peaked, drizzle in the saffron syrup and continue mixing until fairly stiff peaks form and it is the desired consistency for a topping on the cake.

ALTERNATIVE: Serve the saffron scented-whipped cream on top of a cup of hot chocolate infused with a shot of Spanish brandy while snuggling in front of the fireplace.

An Easter Brunch

Easter week is a big deal in Spain. During Semana Santa, Sevilla and many other towns shut down for the week and hold religious processions through their streets. Easter ends the fasting of Semana Santa and Lent. In Portugal, where there is no Easter Bunny tradition, many people eat rabbit. Baby lamb is also popular, and decorative sweet breads, *Folar da Páscoa*, are prepared with hard-boiled eggs pressed into the top before they are baked.

Easter Music
Andalucian Saeta or Flamenco Guitar
The music of Semana Santa is as serious as its subject: the crucifixion. The central song is the Saeta. Sung from balconies to the processions of penitents below, it starts with a moan, descends into a lament and ends in a groan. Often grouped with this music is *Misas Flamencas*, flamenco music that is performed in a religious context.

There are albums of Semana Santa music and Misa Flamenca. On his album *Sketches in Spain*, Miles Davis introduced the Saeta into the American Jazz vernacular. But if you prefer something lighter, there are many flamenco guitar albums to choose from. Consider works by the following masters: Sabicas (1912–1990), Paco de Lucía (1947–) or Tomatito (1958–), who span three generations of flamenco guitar.

Cava Mimosa

SERVES 1

2 ounces Brut Cava
6 ounces fresh orange juice

1 Pour the cava into a chilled glass, add the juice, and lightly stir to mix.

Spanish Bloody Mary

SERVES 1

2 ounces Fino Sherry
6 ounces Bloody Mary mix

1 Pour the sherry into a glass, add the Bloody Mary mix, and lightly stir to combine.

Chocolate and Churros

SERVES 4

1 teaspoon flour, rice flour, or cornstarch
1 tablespoon warm water
2 cups milk
10 ounces semisweet chocolate powder

Spanish hot chocolate is so thick that it is more of a pudding than a drink. It is served with churros, deep fried sticks of batter. If you don't have any churros, cake donuts will work in a pinch.

1 Dissolve the flour in the warm water. When dissolved, whisk in the milk and the chocolate. Heat to boiling, whisking continuously, lifting from burner as it reaches a boil. Return to heat and repeat twice more. The chocolate should become quite thick.

CHURROS

Churros are popular street food sold from special trucks parked anywhere there is a *feria*, and at cafes that sell nothing else, just chocolate y churros. The dough is squeezed out of a press suspended over a vast tub of boiling oil in the form of a spiral. When one side is done, it is flipped over and cooked until both sides are golden brown. Then it is removed to a counter where it is snipped into pieces with shears, wrapped in paper cones, and sold by weight. No one ever claims churros are healthy, just that they are delicious.

Baby Shrimp Meat–Stuffed Eggs

MAKES 24 TAPAS

$1/4$ teaspoon sweet smoked
    pimentón
$1/2$ cup mayonnaise
$1/2$ pound baby shrimp meat
1 dozen hard-boiled eggs
12 lemon-stuffed olives, cut in half
    lengthwise for garnish

1 Combine the first 3 ingredients. Half the eggs and remove the yolks, reserving for another use. Fill the cavity in the egg halves with the shrimp mixture. Top with an olive.

VARIATIONS
Use hummus, tuna salad, or any other salad that will work as a filling.

Egg Yolk Romesco Montaditos

MAKES 24 TAPAS

12 hard-boiled egg yolks
$1/4$ cup Romesco (page 109)
$1/2$ cup Alioli (page 111)
Pinch salt
Grind black pepper
24 slices small baguette
24 ripe olives, pitted, optional
2 tablespoons minced parsley,
    optional

At this point you are looking at a dozen leftover egg yolks. Use them to make Montaditos, two dozen little open-faced sandwiches.

1 In a large yellow mortar, mash the yolks, Romesco, and Alioli into a paste, and then stir in the salt and pepper. Cover each of the bread slices with this mixture. Top with an olive or sprinkle with minced parsley.

Fried Piquillo Pepper Montaditos

MAKES 10 TAPAS

1 jar whole piquillo peppers
(usually 10)
2 tablespoons flour
1 tablespoon sweet Spanish
pimentón
Pinch fine sea salt
1 egg, beaten
1/2 cup olive oil
10 to 18 slices French bread (ovals
about 3-inches wide will fit best
under the piquillos)

We were wandering around Bilbao one morning and ducked into a bar for some coffee. Basque cooks are very inventive and even in this little place they had put a new twist on breakfast. This is one of the tapas they were serving at that hour of day.

1 Drain the peppers.

2 Mix the flour, pimentón, and salt together, and dip the piquillos first into this mixture, then into the egg. Heat the oil and then fry, turning once. Serve on a slice of fresh bread.

Membrillo and Manchego Montaditos

MAKES 24 TAPAS

1/2 cup olive oil
24 slices baguette
1/2 pound Manchego, cut into 24
triangular slices
8 ounces membrillo (quince paste),
cut into matching triangles

Membrillo and manchego are a classic pairing and will contribute a little toward the satisfaction of the sweet tooths in attendance. In Portugal the same pairing, queijo e marmelada, is called "Romeo and Juliet."

1 Heat the oil until it hazes. Drop a small piece of bread into the oil, it should sizzle and begin to brown immediately. Fry a few pieces of the baguette at a time, turning once to brown evenly on both sides, and remove with a slotted spoon. Top each slice with a slice of cheese, and then top the cheese with a slice of membrillo.

Tortilla Española

SERVES 10

1 onion, minced
Olive oil
3 potatoes, peeled and thinly sliced
5 to 6 eggs, beaten
2 to 3 teaspoons fine sea salt

This is the classic tapa, morning, noon, and night. It is a hard-cooked omelet, which can be cut into cubes and served with toothpicks, cut into wedges to be served with a fork, or placed between halves of a split baguette for a *bocadillo*, a great breakfast sandwich. Traditionally, tortillas are made by cooking the mixture in a hot pan and flipping it over several times using a plate as an aid. This recipe makes the tortilla in a microwave, which is complete heresy.

1 Place onions in a 10-inch cazuela with enough oil to cover them and microwave until soft, about 3–4 minutes. Mix in the sliced potatoes and microwave until easily pierced with a fork, approximately 10–15 minutes.

2 Mix the eggs and salt, and pour over the potatoes pressing down on them so they are covered by the egg mixture. Microwave 5–6 minutes until the top is cooked. The middle and the bottom will still be eggy. Run a knife around the edge of the tortilla and jiggle it to make sure it doesn't stick, then flip it onto a plate. Microwave another 3–5 minutes until done. Slice into ten wedges after letting it rest for a few minutes.

VARIATION Split the recipe in two and make a layer cake tortilla with sauce between the layers and over the top.

MONTADITOS For tapas, use the single layers as bases for montaditos. Top with white asparagus, a slice of sobrasada, a square of red pepper, and spear with a toothpick to stabilize.

CLASSIC TORTILLA ESPAÑOLA

The secret of a classic tortilla española is to use lots of olive oil and to use lots of salt. Do not brown the potatoes; let them simmer in the oil until they are soft without burning. Finally, we use a nonstick frying pan that is the size you want the tortilla to be, filling it with potatoes and burying them to the rim in beaten eggs. The tricky part is when you get to learn how to flip the tortilla onto a plate and then slide it back into the pan. A word of advice: This is something you should do for the first time in private.

Easter Brunch Bread

Making bread is an easy, if slightly long, process, but the actual time you are working on it is minimal as there are long breaks while it rises. This fluffy loaf has a sprinkling of flavors I associate with Spain.

MAKES 1 LOAF

SPONGE
1/2 cup flour
1/2 cup warm water
1 package dry yeast
1 tablespoon orange blossom
  honey

DOUGH
1 cup milk, at room temperature
1/4 pound butter, melted
1/2 teaspoon salt
2 large eggs
1/8 cup minced orange zest
1/8 cup poppy seeds
1/4 cup toasted pine nuts
3 1/2 cups flour

SPONGE

1 Combine the ingredients and proof 30 minutes until bubbles form.

DOUGH
2 Mix together all of the ingredients, adding the flour 1/2 cup at a time.

3 Turn out onto a board and knead until elastic. I like to watch a music station on television while I work. It takes about three songs. The dough will be quite wet, so keep your hands floured and work the dough with a pastry scraper. Oil a large bowl and turn the dough into it, turning it over so the oiled side is up. Let rise until doubled in volume, about 45 minutes, depending on the room temperature.

4 Preheat oven to 350 degrees F.

5 Punch the dough down and form into a loaf. It is very flexible. I make a U shape and twist the two arms over each other. Place on a baking sheet sprinkled with cornmeal.

5 Let rise again about 40 minutes. Bake 40 minutes.

Scrambled Eggs with Ground Pork and Pimentón

SERVES 6

¼ cup Spanish olive oil
1 yellow onion, finely chopped
2 cloves garlic, finely chopped
1 pound ground pork
2 tablespoons hot Spanish pimentón
10 eggs, beaten

The Spanish love scrambled eggs and eat them often with any meal of the day. Many times a small portion of some local ingredient is lightly scrambled with just a little egg to bind it and served as a tapa. This is a hearty version.

1 Heat the oil in a large frying pan. Add the onion and garlic and cook until limp. Add the pork and brown, breaking it up with a spatula as it cooks. Add pimentón and toss to incorporate. Add the eggs and cook until done.

Strawberries Marinated in PX Vinegar

SERVES 10

1 quart strawberries
⅛ cup sugar
1 teaspoon PX or aged sherry vinegar

Strawberries are ripe by Easter in Barcelona, the full-sized *fresas* or the tiny wild *fresitas*. Perfect specimens of them are proudly displayed in all the markets and restaurants. This is a very Spanish way to serve them. The vinegar draws out the juice in the strawberries, which blends with the sugar to coat them with a natural syrup. If served as a tapa, spear each berry with a toothpick before serving them. ☙ This recipe is adapted from one on the Power-Selles company Web site, a company formed by my friends Betsy Powers and Pere Selles to import specialty gourmet foods from Spain.

1 Wash and drain the strawberries and place them in a dish. Sprinkle the berries with sugar and then with vinegar. Let stand for 2–3 hours.

Wine Tastings

Wine Tastings

A good time to have a wine tasting is in the early spring. That is when the wine bodegas of Spain and Portugal begin to change the vintage of the wines they are shipping to the United States. It is also before *Wine Spectator and Parker* start to publish their reviews and you can form your own opinions. The pros swirl, sniff, suck, and spit without swallowing. I recommend taking more time, actually drinking the wines, having a little food, revisiting the wines again after both they, and you, have had a chance to breathe and relax.

So gather some like-minded compatriots around the dining room table. Taste the wines blind by putting the bottles in paper bags and then removing the corks and neck caps. Assign each bag a letter from the alphabet. Labeling the bottles "a" thru "f" reduces the confusion of referring to both the ranking and the bottle by number. Then start tasting. Hand out some kind of score sheets for the categories of color, aroma, taste, finish, score, group ranking and label. After tasting the wines, have everyone rank them in the order of preference with number one being best. Add up the scores. The lowest score "wins."

Wines

Wine-Tasting Music
The Tango

Initially, everyone is nervous at a scored wine tasting as if it were their tastes, rather than the wine's taste, that is being ranked. Argentine tango shares this nervousness. It came off the docks of Buenos Aires with an edgy attitude that it retains today. If you want to hear tango the old fashioned way it was originally presented, buy a CD collecting the works of the late Carlos Gardel (1887–1935). But it was Astor Piazolla (1921–1992) who fused tango with jazz and developed Tango Nuevo, a sound that still seems contemporary. For tango that is completely contemporary, listen to the electonica-influenced tracks of the group Gotan Project. For sacred tango, *Misa Tango* by Luis Bacalov is performed by Plácido Domingo and Ana Maria Martinez with an orchestra and choir.

Choosing the Wines

Six to eight wines is a good number to taste and enjoy without becoming overwhelmed. Whether you ask everyone to bring a wine or one person picks them all, there are different ways to set the parameters for a blind tasting:

By Varietal: Tempranillo, Garnacha, Mencia, Tinto Roriz, etc.

By Region: Rioja, Ribera del Duero, Toro, Alentejo, etc.

Vertically: Different vintages of the same wine. In Rioja, this is easy; you just need a Crianza, Reserva, and Gran Reserva.

Specialty Wines: Try blind tasting cavas, Spain's sparkling wines, or espumantes from Portugal. Or try tasting the fortified wines: madeiras, ports, and sherries. With fortified wines, consider whether your audience will be the uninitiated or sophisticated in deciding whether your selection should be an introduction to the range of styles or one that delves into the subtleties within a type.

Food Pairing: Choose a menu, then judge wines on how they pair with leg of lamb or fish roasted in garlic sauce, etc.

Temperature: One interesting tasting experiment is to serve the same red wine at three temperatures: 55 degrees F, 65 degrees F, and 75 degrees F.

Blending: After the conventional tasting, try blending to your own palate with the leftover wines. For example, mix a little softer structured wine into a very tannic wine.

Spanish Reds (tinto)
The major Spanish red wine regions, which have in recent years proliferated, are:
- Rioja
- Navarra
- Bierzo (Galicia)
- Ribera del Duero
- Toro
- La Mancha/Valdepañas
- Priorat/Montsant/Terra Alta
- Jumilla

Major Spanish red wine grape varietals are:
- Tempranillo
- Graciano
- Mazuelo (Carignan)
- Garnacha (Grenache)
- Monastrell (Mourvèdere)
- Mencia

Spanish nomenclature for aging:
- Tinto: generally a young red that has not been barrel aged.
- Barrica: a barrel-aged wine that does not meet the specifications for Crianza.
- Crianza: the established system of barrel-and bottle-aging wine so that it is released 2 years after the harvest, having spent 6 months in barrels.
- Reservas: a combined 3 years of aging prior to release.
- Gran Reservas: must be the most structured of a Rioja bodega's wines as it is released no less than 5 years after the harvest. If the wines from a vintage are unsuitable for aging, most bodegas will not make a Gran Reserva that year. There is a web of gold wire on traditional bottles of Gran Reseva.
- Renegades: most Rioja bodegas are making a "modern" wine, huge, extracted, and heavily oaked. These are referred to by the wineries as, *"Propriedad," "Selección,"* or *"Vino de Autor."*

Spanish Whites (blanco)
Spanish whites often got a bad rap in older wine books before stainless steel and temperature-controlled fermentation revolutionized the industry. Today, Spain's white wines can compete with those of any other country. Here are the major white wine regions and the grapes that predominate within them:

Pais Basque: Txomin and Txakoli (Hondarrabi Zuri)
A dry, spritzy wine served unfiltered in Basque bars but refined for bottling.

Galicia: Albariño
Crisp and dry with floral, peachy, and lychee nut aromas; medium bodied and a perfect match for fish.

White Rioja: Viura
The quality of wines from this grape has improved so drastically that most wine books are completely out of date in rating it. White Riojas are truly one of the greatest values in the wine world.

Rueda: Verdejo
This native grape was almost extinct; its popularity has seen a resurgence in Spain. Wines made from it are marked by hints of grapefruit in the nose and delightful herbal notes on the palate, qualities that make it easy to serve with summer salads.

Sauvignon Blanc
Technically this is a French grape, but it thrives in Rueda where it is bottled both as a varietal and blended with Verdejo.

Catalonian Whites (Penedès)
The white grapes of this area are the same grapes traditionally used for cava, Macabeo (Viura in Rioja), Xarel-lo and Parellada. There have also been "experimental" plantings of both Chardonnay and Pinot Noir,

French grapes grown by those cava bodegas desiring to more closely emulate champagne.

Portuguese Wine Grapes
The Portuguese wine Denomination of Origins (DOCs) and regions seem to me slightly less clearly organized than the Spanish. The wine grapes are numerous and for the most part, unique to Portugal. Some of them are the same grape graced with a regional name. This is a simplistic overview:

Regions (north to south)
• Vinho Verde
• Douro
• Dão
• Bairrada
• Ribatejo
• Alentejo

Tinto/Red
In the north, the port wine grape growers have recently focused on five varieties out of over twenty traditionally grown. You will find table wines bottled under these varietal names as well as blends of these grapes. These grapes are also grown in the Dão and Bairrada albeit sometimes under different names:
• Touriga Nacional
• Tinta Roriz is the same grape as the Spanish Tempranillo
• Touriga Francesa
• Tinto Cão
• Tinta da Barca

In the south, some other grape names you will encounter include:

• Aragonez (tempranillo)
• Periquita
• Trincadeira Preta
• Alfrocheiro Preto

Branco/White:
Among the myriad grapes grown in Portugal for dry, white table wines, remember these two:
• Alvarinho: the same grape as the Galician Albariño, this internationally recognized grape is grown across the northern part of the Vinho Verde region (confusingly enough, there is a red vinho verde in Portugal). The wine has depth and body and wonderful aromas.
• Malvasia Fina: this grape can be used to make a sweet wine, but when all the sugar is fermented, it makes a delightful, quaffable dry white.

Wine Tasting Menu Items
It challenges not just wine but your taste buds to match strong-tasting food with wines when you are trying to focus on the subtleties of the wines. So while actively tasting, tend to stay away from vinegars, anchovies, and garlic-dominated foods. This does not apply to any meal that follows.

While tasting, at a minimum serve some bread to cleanse the pallet as well as water to refresh it. But something a little more substantial is hospitable. We are not talking about a wine dinner, so elaborate food is not expected, but a little sustenance is nice. Here are some simple ideas.

Fried Marcona Almonds

1 cup olive oil
1/2 **pound Marcona almonds,
blanched**
Sprinkle Spanish sea salt

Marcona almonds can be expensive, but they are worth the price if you are as nuts about nuts as I am. If you use regular almonds, frying them in olive oil still enhances their flavor.

1 Heat olive oil to frying temperature. When it hazes, drop one nut in to test. It should immediately sizzle in the oil, sweating a little bubble of moisture. If it just sits there, wait a little longer before adding the rest of the nuts.

2 Fry the nuts, stirring them to promote even browning. When golden in color, remove with a slotted spoon. Drain and salt.

Jamón Lollipops

18 ounces jamón serrano
1 package (4 ounces) bread sticks

This ultra-simple tapa is a good test of a wine because if a wine does not complement jamón, it is only suitable for Sangría.

1 Wrap thin slices of the jamón around the top two-thirds of the bread sticks for "lollipops."

Flank Steak Piri Piri Montaditos

MAKES 24 TAPAS

1 pound flank steak
$1/4$ cup Piri Piri Sauce (page 107)
Pinch coarse sea salt
24 slices of a baguette
$1/4$ cup mayonnaise

Hot sauce does not give most wines a chance to show their subtleties, but here, after grilling, the Piri Piri Sauce is only a background note. It will not overpower the wine being tasted and provides a wine a chance to show if it has the character to be paired with red meat.

1 Brush the steak with the sauce on both sides, then dust it with coarse sea salt. Grill or broil until medium rare. Let cool.

2 Slice and cut steak into pieces no larger than the baguette slices. Brush each slice of bread with a little mayonnaise and add a slice of meat to complete the montadito.

Cold Green Beans with Pine Nuts and Spanish Blue Cheese

MAKES 8 TAPAS

$1/2$ pound green beans, cut in 1-inch lengths
Pinch salt
Water
1 tablespoon Cabrales or Valdeón or other Spanish blue cheese
2 tablespoons extra virgin olive oil
1 tablespoon toasted pine nuts

1 Cook the green beans *al dente* in boiling salted water and then drain. Crumble the blue cheese and work the olive oil into it using the tines of a fork. Toss with beans, then sprinkle with the nuts. Serve at room temperature.

Portuguese Corn Bread

MAKES ONE 2-POUND LOAF OF
DENSE COUNTRY BREAD

THE SPONGE
1 package dry yeast
$^1/_2$ cup cornmeal
$^1/_2$ cup warm water

THE DOUGH
$^1/_2$ cup beer, at room temperature
$^1/_2$ cup warm milk
$^1/_8$ cup extra virgin olive oil
1 teaspoon salt
1$^1/_2$ cups cornmeal, divided
2 cups unbleached flour
4 ounces Palhais goat cheese,
   grated, optional

American corn bread is a quick bread made by pouring a batter containing baking powder in a pan and baking it. It is crumbly rather than chewy. This is yeast bread, which uses cornmeal in place of about one-third of the flour. It is rough and hearty and pairs well with cheese and wine.

THE SPONGE

1 In a large warm bowl, combine the ingredients, stirring them to form a batter. Cover and let proof in a warm, but not hot, place until the surface is broken by myriad bubbles and the batter has turned into a light and spongy mass. This should take about 30 minutes and you should have about twice the mass you started with. Don't worry if it smells like a backwoods corn-mash still. That is just the yeast doing its thing with the corn.

THE DOUGH

2 When the sponge is ready, add the first 4 ingredients and 1 cup of the cornmeal. Stir to form a batter. Now work in the flour, $^1/_2$ cup at a time. By the time you are done you should have stiff but finger-friendly dough.

3 Turn it out onto a board dusted with cornmeal and knead it for 5–10 minutes until you feel it become elastic. It will be sticky, so keep dusting your hands and the dough with the reserved cornmeal. Remember that this is corn bread and that it will continue to feel like rough cloth, not silken as some dough does. When the dough has responded to your prodding, shape it into a ball.

4 Rinse and dry the bowl. Pour a little olive oil in it and put the ball of dough in the bowl and turn it over, oiled side up. Cover and let rise until doubled in bulk, about 1 hour. Turn the ball out, and punch it down. Sprinkle the cheese over the surface and knead it for 5 minutes. Return to re-oiled bowl for a second rise.

5 When it has doubled in bulk, punch and knead it another 5 minutes and form it into any shape loaf you like and cover it with waxed paper to keep it cozy and warm.

6 While the dough is rising for the third time, preheat the oven to 500 degrees F. Place a pan in the bottom of the oven for water. If you use a baking stone, place it on the center rack. Place the risen loaf on a baking sheet dusted with corn-meal to prevent sticking. Slash the top if you like. Slide it in the oven and carefully add water to the hot pan to make lots of steam. Bake 15 minutes.

7 Reduce heat to 400 degrees F, adding more water to the pan. Bake another 15 minutes. The bread will be done when you knock on it and the loaf sounds hollow.

Savory Gypsy's Arm

MAKES TWO 1¹/2-POUND LOAVES

2 packages dry yeast
2 cups warm water
2 tablespoons sugar
$^1/_4$ cup extra virgin olive oil
1 tablespoon salt
6 cups unbleached flour, divided
$^1/_2$ cup Olivada (page 110)
$^1/_2$ cup toasted pine nuts
$^1/_2$ cup currants, soaked in hot
   water to plump them up

In Spain, Gypsy's Arm is usually a rolled cake with a sweet filling. When the rolls are sliced into servings, the pieces show off a lovely pattern of concentric rings.

1 Dissolve the yeast in the warm water and let stand 5 minutes. Stir in the sugar, oil, and salt and work in 5 cups of the flour, $^1/_2$ cup at a time. Turn out onto a floured board and knead, dusting your hands and the dough with flour from the sixth cup. Let rest 10 minutes and knead again, continuing to add flour. When the dough is smooth and elastic, form it into a ball. Put some olive oil in the bottom of a bowl twice the size of your ball of dough. Put the dough in the bowl and flip it over so the oiled side is up. Cover and let rise in a warm place until doubled in bulk, about 1 hour.

2 Turn the dough back out onto your floured board, punch down, and knead briefly. Cut the dough into two portions. Roll each half into a rectangle 15 x 8 inches.

Spread the Olivada over the surface of the first loaf to within 1 inch of the far side, then roll up the rectangle away from you to form a long loaf, pressing the edge to seal it. Sprinkle the second loaf with the nuts and currants, and roll the same way as the first loaf. I like to slash the tops with my pastry razor.

3 Preheat oven to 500 degrees F if a rustic crust is desired, and to 375 degrees F for a conventional crust.

4 While the oven heats, let the loaves rise again until doubled in bulk, about 30 minutes. For a rustic, thick crust, bake for a total of 30 minutes, 15 minutes at 500 degrees F with steam and then 15 minutes at 400 degrees F (see steps 5 and 6 on facing page). For a conventional crust, bake 40 minutes at 375 degrees F in a dry oven.

Barbecuing the Spanish Table Style

One of the pleasures of cazuelas is that they can go right on the barbecue grill. This means that a side dish of beans can be burbling away or that you can use them to braise meat, starting it over the coals, then moving it to a cazuela and finishing it with a bit of wine. Cataplanas can also be set over hot coals. Spanish and Portuguese sausages, from Basque chorizo to Catalan butifarrita, lend themselves to being grilled and served with a bun.

Barbecue Music
Cuban Son

There is a treasure trove of son available from historic recordings to contemporary bands. You can not go wrong with individual CDs by the Buena Vista Club artists, from the late pianist Rubén González, singers Compay Segundo and Ibrahim Ferrer to diva Omara Portuondo, or percussionist Cachaito.

Son traveled back to Spain and some of its rhythms and ideas were incorporated into flamenco, a process that continues today. If you are curious about this, listen to Son de la Frontera or to Lágrimas Negras, which pairs flamenco vocalist Cigala with Cuban son pianist Bebo Valdéz (jazz pianist Chucho Valdéz's father).

Fino Sherry and Melon Aguafresca

MAKES 12 (8-OUNCE) GLASSES

1 ripe melon (cantaloupe, honeydew, or other melon of similar
size), seeded and peeled, then
chilled
1 lemon, squeezed
1 bottle Fino sherry, chilled
Mint sprigs for garnish, optional

This drink tastes of summer and is always refreshing.

1 Purée chilled melon in a blender, add lemon juice, and chill until ready to use.

2 To make by the glass, combine 2 ounces of the sherry with 6 ounces of the melon purée, and garnish with a sprig of mint.

3 You can also make this by the pitcher. Using the same ratio of 2 ounces of sherry to 6 ounces of melon purée per glass, pour into a pitcher, combine, and top each glass with a sprig of mint as served.

Peaches and Cherries Sangría

SERVES 4

3 peaches, sliced
1 pound pitted cherries
1 bottle (750 milliliters) white
wine, chilled
1 (12 ounce) can lemon-lime soda,
chilled
4 sprigs mint, for garnish, optional

This combination is a summer delight. If fresh peaches or fresh cherries are not available the day of your barbecue, use frozen fruit and it will work just fine.

1 Place peaches and cherries in a 1½ liter pitcher and muddle gently with a wooden pestle to release juices. Add the wine and soda and serve over ice cubes. Garnish with a sprig of mint.

Prawns and Linguiça Skewers

MAKES 6 SKEWERS

1 pound (18–25 count) large
prawns
1/2 pound linguiça cut into 1/4-inch-
thick slices

This is a favorite summer barbecue treat.

1 Skewer the prawns, each with a linguiça slice skewered from the side, so the prawn curls around the coin-like slice. Grill over hot coals, letting the fatty juices from the linguiça bathe the prawns, until the prawns are opaque and the linguiça is crisp.

Chorizo and Mushroom Skewers

MAKES 20–24 TAPAS

24 bamboo skewers
1 pound Spanish-style cooking
  chorizo, cut in 1/2-inch chunks
24 crimini mushroom caps (match
  their size to the diameter of the
  chorizo)
12 Spanish bay leaves
1 bottle (750 milliliters) Spanish
  red table wine

These skewers can be made with slices of chorizo or little cocktail-size chorizo called *cantimpalitos*. Marinating in wine adds complexity to the flavors.

1 Place 1 mushroom cap and 2 chorizo pieces on each skewer.

2 Put the bay leaves in the bottom of a shallow container large enough to hold skewers. Lay the skewers on top then add the red wine to cover. If there is not enough wine to completely cover the skewers, make sure you turn them once or twice while they are marinating.

Marinate several hours or overnight. Drain and grill, broil, or bake in a hot oven (425–450 degrees F) until the chorizo is hot through to center and starts to sizzle.

NOTE: If you skip the marinating step, be sure to soak the bamboo skewers in water so they do not burn on the grill.

Madeiran Beef Skewers

MAKES 6 SKEWERS

MARINADE
6 bay leaves
6 cloves garlic, roughly chopped
1/2 cup Madeira
1/8 cup wine vinegar

SKEWERS
1 teaspoon salt
Grind black pepper
1 1/2 pounds beef tenderloin, cut
  into 1-inch cubes
Pinch extra coarse sea salt
1/4 cup butter

In Madeira, the skewers are sticks cut from fresh bay limbs. Unless you have a bay tree growing in your yard, you will have to use metal skewers.

MARINADE
1 Combine the ingredients to create a marinade.

SKEWERS
2 Salt and pepper the beef cubes, then marinate the meat for 1–2 hours.

3 Drain the beef cubes and thread them on a skewer, allowing them to come to room temperature while getting the coal briquettes started and ready for grilling.

4 Dust the skewers with sea salt and grill them over the hot coals. Remove from the grill, giving them a good knock to dislodge extra sea salt. Place on a platter and brush them on all sides with the butter.

NOTE: If you use wooden skewers, soak them in water prior to using. This will prevent them from burning.

Madeiran Fried Polenta Cubes

The Madieran Beef Skewers (page 163) are traditionally served with *milho*, polenta flaked with parsley leaves that are cubed and fried.

page 163

SERVES 6

3 cups boiling water or chicken stock
1/2 teaspoon sea salt
1/2 cup minced parsley
1 cup polenta
1 cup olive oil

1 Bring the water to a boil and stir in the salt, parsley, and polenta. Return to a boil and cook according to the instructions on polenta, from 1–20 minutes depending on the type of polenta, stirring constantly. Pour into a 8-inch square pan, or the equivalent, to make a 1-inch-thick layer. When cool, cut into 1-inch square cubes.

2 Heat the oil to a haze. Fry the polenta cubes in batches until they start to brown. Remove with a slotted spoon.

Butifarra with Beans Fried in Olive Oil

For each serving, use this list as a multiplication table. ⟋ If you want to get fancy, grill a quartered rabbit, too. It is one of the things we do when we get homesick for Catalonia.

SERVES 1

1 cup plus 1 tablespoon olive oil, divided
2 butifarra (Catalan white sausages)
1 cup cooked white beans, drained of all their moisture
Sprinkle coarse sea salt

1 Heat 1 tablespoon oil in a cazuela. Prick the sausages so their juice can escape, and fry them to a golden brown. Remove the sausages from the cazuela and keep warm.

2 Add the remaining olive oil to the cazuela, heating until it hazes. Add the beans and fry until their skins crisp. Remove using a slotted spoon and drain of any excess oil. Sprinkle with salt.

3 Once you have eaten beans this way, you will discover an alternative to french fries. They pair perfectly with any grilled meat.

NOTE: To avoid spattering, the cooked beans should be free of moisture. I drain them and lay them out on a baking sheet to dry prior to frying.

Sherry-Braised Rabbit

SERVES 4

2 tablespoons butter
2 cloves garlic, crushed
1 yellow onion, diced
Pinch salt
Grind black pepper
1 rabbit, quartered, or 4 hind
   quarters
1¹/₂ cups dry Amontillado sherry

Rabbit, *conejo*, can go on the grill just rubbed with garlic and then dusted with coarse sea salt. Brush a little olive oil over it as it roasts and serve with a bowl of alioli on the side. But here is a variation adapted for the barbecue from the signature dish Amy McCray prepares at Eva Restaurant, serving it with Chorizo Bread Pudding (page 125). Braising is one of the techniques cocotes and ollas are handy for since they can be used on the grill.

1 Over a bed of hot coals, melt butter in a large cocote or olla, then brown the garlic and onion. Move the cocote to a cooler part of the grill. Sprinkle salt and pepper over the rabbit, then brown pieces on both sides over hot coals. Put the browned pieces in the cocote and pour the sherry over the rabbit and cover the cocote. Then cover the barbecue to keep in the moisture and the heat. Let simmer 1 hour, turning the rabbit over once. Open the barbecue and remove the cocote lid and let cooking liquid reduce by ¹/₂ to a thick sauce. Serve the rabbit with the reduced cooking liquids.

Grilled Swordfish, Pirate Style

SERVES 4

¹/₂ teaspoon fresh rosemary
¹/₂ teaspoon pebrella
¹/₂ teaspoon coarse Spanish sea
   salt
2 tablespoons olive oil
¹/₄ lemon
2 pounds swordfish steak

SAUCE
2 tablespoons extra virgin olive oil
3 cloves garlic, sliced
¹/₄ cup dry white wine
2 tablespoons Spanish capers

A former employee of The Spanish Table was known to the staff as *La Pirata*. This is her recipe.

1 Place the herbs and salt in a mortar and grind them together with a pestle.

2 Slowly add the oil, then squeeze in the juice of the lemon. Brush this mixture over the fish and allow to rest while grill is heating. Grill the fish 4 minutes per side.

SAUCE
3 While fish is grilling, place a cazuela to one side of the grill, adding the olive oil and garlic and letting it cook until it is a deep almond brown. Then add the wine, capers, and finally the grilled fish, heating through before serving.

Grilled Artichokes Bathed in Olivada

SERVES 4

2 large artichokes or a dozen baby
  artichokes
Water to cover
4 cloves garlic, finely chopped
1/4 cup olive oil
1/4 cup Olivada (page 110)
1 teaspoon salt
1/4 lemon

Artichokes, both large and baby, can be split and grilled, after being parboiled. The charred flavor of the grilled artichoke leaves curl up ever so comfortably to the rich, earthy flavor of the Black Olivada. These ingredients have been used in Spain since Roman times.

1 Cook the artichokes in boiling water until the bottom can be pierced with a fork. Drain and let cool to a comfortable temperature. When they can be handled, split them in half lengthwise and remove the choke with a spoon.

2 While coals are heating, slowly cook the garlic in the oil. When the garlic is soft, stir in the Olivada and set aside.

3 Place the split artichokes face down over the hot coals and cook until brown and the leaves start to curl. Turn over onto their backs and drizzle the garlic oil-Olivada mixture over the cut side. Grill until brown on the back side. Sprinkle with salt and drizzle with lemon as you serve.

White Bean and Pasta Salad

SERVES 2–4

2 cups cooked white beans
1 cup cooked small shell-shaped
  pasta
2 scallions, trimmed and chopped,
  green tops and all
1 red bell pepper, finely diced
2 tablespoons minced cilantro
2 tablespoons lemon juice
1/4 cup alioli
1 hard-boiled egg, finely chopped
1 tin North Atlantic Bonito Tuna
  packed in olive oil, optional
Pinch salt
Grind black pepper

Beans should show up at the table as often as possible. Not just because they are filled with nutrition, but because they taste great. Adding the tuna makes this a hearty main-dish salad, but you can omit it if you want to keep it lighter. The pasta complicates the texture, but it is a mere fillip. The egg, which may seem extraneous, binds the dressing.

1 Mix all the ingredients in a bowl.
Add salt and pepper, to taste.

Braised Pork Tenderloin

SERVES 6

2 (2-pound) pork tenderloins
2 tablespoons Pincho Seasoning, red or yellow (page 106)
$1/4$ cup olive oil
$1/2$ cup wine, red if using red pincho seasoning, white if using yellow
1 lemon

In this recipe, pork tenderloin is dry rubbed with pincho seasoning, then braised in an open cazuela. The liquid keeps the meat moist while it absorbs flavor from the smoke. Pork tenderloin is one of the ways you can reward yourself after a hard day's work. For a tapa, the slices can be made into mini-sandwiches.

1 The day before, place each tenderloin on a sheet of plastic wrap and dust with pincho seasoning, turning to ensure complete coverage. Wrap tightly and refrigerate overnight.

2 When barbecue coals are hot, sear tenderloins on all sides on the grill. When browned, put in a cazuela with the oil and turn to coat. Add the wine and close the cover on barbecue. Cook 20–30 minutes until the internal temperature is 160 degrees F, turning every 10 minutes to ensure even cooking. Remove from cazuela and let cool slightly before slicing. Leave the cazuela on the grill, allowing the cooking liquid reduce by $1/2$ to form a sauce. Slice meat just before serving. Squeeze a few drops of lemon juice over the cut meat and serve with pan juices.

GRILLED MEAT

Grilled meat is an essential element of Spanish cuisine and one of the reasons traditionally structured Spanish wines such as Riojas are slightly acidic. This style of wine, in contrast to fruit-forward more syrupy wines, cleanses the palate of fats from the meat and refreshes the taste buds.

Japanese eggplants
Ripe bell peppers
Sweet onions
Firm tomatoes
Potatoes
Olive oil
Finely chopped fresh garlic
Arbequina extra virgin olive oil
Coarse sea salt

**SOME VEGETABLES TO
CONSIDER**

Onions
Green and red bell peppers
Zucchini
Eggplant
Asparagus
Long or green beans
Green onions or leeks
Olive oil
Extra coarse sea salt
Garlic, minced
Romesco (page 109)

Escalivada (Fire-Roasted Whole Vegetables)

Escalivada is whole vegetables that are placed on a fire's hot coals to cook until they are charred. You often see this cooking technique used on red peppers, but the Catalans combine the peppers with eggplants, onions, potatoes, and even firm tomatoes, letting their juices, and flavors, mingle. You can also prepare escalivada by brushing the whole vegetables with oil and roasting them in a cazuela in a very hot oven, 450 degrees F, turning them occasionally, until they turn black. The chopped garlic is crunchy, a nice contrast to the limpness of the roasted vegetables, but if its flavor is too strong for you, use garlic stewed in olive oil.

1 Brush vegetables with olive oil and lay them on a hot grill until they are charred black. Turn them to char on all sides evenly. When black, put them in a paper bag to steam until they are cool enough to handle. Then pull off the charred skins and tear the moist inner flesh into strips.

2 Sprinkle garlic over the strips, drizzle with oil, and dust with sea salt.

Grilled Vegetables

For escalivada, vegetables are cooked until they collapse. An alternative is to quickly grill slices of fresh vegetable basted with garlic olive oil. Seared over a hot fire, the fresh vegetables gain a smoky richness.

1 Cut the vegetables into thick slices, brush them with oil and sprinkle them with coarse sea salt. Use coarse salt, or extra coarse sea salt, because it does not melt in the flames. Use salt before cooking because it draws out the vegetable sugars and speeds caramelization.

2 Grill them until they are striped with black grill lines but are still al dente to the touch of the barbecue fork. Remove them to a warm platter, sprinkle with raw garlic and drizzle a little extra virgin olive oil over them or serve them with some Romesco sauce.

Grilled Vegetable Salad with Xató Dressing

SERVES 4

XATÓ DRESSING
2 tablespoons red wine vinegar
2 tablespoons Romesco (page 109)
1/4 cup extra virgin olive oil

One head lettuce of choice
Grilled vegetables

Xató (a Romesco-based dressing) is often served with bitter greens such as escarole, but it is also great on sweet lettuces. Use either as a bed in this salad. You will need some of the Grilled Vegetables (facing) split into four portions to place over the fresh greens.

1 Combine the dressing ingredients and then toss with the greens. Divide onto individual salad plates and place grilled vegetables on top.

If someone comes around with a black pepper grinder, you can say yes or no. It is really up to you.

Blackberry-Saffron Sorbete

SERVES 4

1 cup blackberry juice
1/4 cup Saffron Syrup (page 112)
1/4 cup simple sugar syrup (see right)
Toasted pine nuts, optional

I keep a cup or two of simple sugar syrup on hand to make sorbet on the spur of the moment. Dissolve one part sugar in one part water, bring to a boil and simmer 10 minutes, and then chill. Wash whatever ripe fruit you are using, chop it up and run it through a food mill to produce a seedless, uniform pulp. Chill the pulp and combine it with the syrup. ✒ This recipe works with any fruit, but if you use a milder-tasting fruit, such as ripe melon, reduce the saffron syrup accordingly. In Spain, frozen fruit syrups are often served in a frozen hollowed-out half of an orange or lemon.

1 Combine and chill first three ingredients and then freeze in an ice cream maker or in a pan in the freezer of your refrigerator, scraping the syrup several times with an olive wood spatula as it freezes. This keeps it from forming a solid block, the spatula substituting for the paddles in an ice cream maker. Top with nuts when serving.

Beach Paella

I want to get you thinking about cooking and serving a paella outdoors.

When you do, the side dishes should be kept to the lighter side as the entree is very filling. So I have suggested several summer salads for you to select from.

Beach Paella Music
Cabo Verdean Music

There is one kind of music that I think harmonizes with the sound of waves more than any other and that is Cabo Verdean. The songs lyrics speak of lost love, of squandered youth, and of passings. Many of the songs just die down at the end, like the dying embers of a beach fire.

One the best known of the Cabo Verdean singers is Cesária Évora who performs barefooted and without moving, relying on her voice to lift the audience. But there are other younger singers following the path she blazed in exporting the music, such as Fancha and María de Barro.

Sangría

Sangría can be a totally spontaneous reaction to the presence of ripe fruit. I just quarter fruit, mostly citrus—limes, oranges, a grapefruit for tartness—and a juicy apple or even a peach when they are in season. I squeeze them as I put them in the pitcher to release the juice, and then add wine. I use red wine, but white wine lovers should feel free to use white (you can even use sparkling cava). Then I put the pitcher in the refrigerator. When ready to serve, I add up to a can of carbonated citrus-flavored soda such as lemon-lime or grapefruit. Then I pour the sangría into glasses filled with ice, adding a slice of fruit as a garnish.

Classic The Spanish Table Sangría Number 1

MAKES 12 (8 OUNCE) GLASSES

1 lime, cut into 4 pieces
1 lemon, cut into 4 pieces
2 oranges, cut into 4 pieces
1 grapefruit, cut into 4 pieces
2 apples, cored, and each cut into 4 pieces
1 magnum (1¹/₂ liter) bottle of wine, red or white
1 can (12-ounces) lemon-lime or grapefruit soda

This is a light, refreshing sangría with a lower alcohol content.

1 Place all of the citrus fruit into a 2-liter pitcher and crush with a pestle.

2 Add the apples and wine. Put in the refrigerator to chill.

3 When ready to serve, add the soda and pour into 8-ounce or larger sangría glasses filled with ice.

Classic The Spanish Table Sangría Number 2

MAKES 12 (8-OUNCE) GLASSES

1¹/₂ liters red wine (use a medium bodied, fruity red)
4 oranges, 3 juiced, 1 sliced
3 lemons, 2 juiced, 1 sliced
¹/₄ cup sugar
¹/₂ cup Spanish brandy
¹/₄ cup orange liqueur such as Grand Marnier or Cointreau
4 cups club soda
1 apple, sliced for garnish

In this version, distilled liquors are added, giving it more alcoholic punch.

1 In a 2-liter pitcher, combine wine, orange and lemon juices and slices, sugar (use more or less depending on the sweetness of the fruit), the brandy, and the orange liquor. Chill for 2 or more hours. When ready to serve, add the club soda. Pour over ice cubes and garnish with an apple slice.

Beach Paella for 40

Cooking paella at the beach or anywhere outdoors gives you an opportunity to use a pan bigger than your kitchen stove. You need a sturdy stand for the paella pan to sit on. It has to be level and can not tip when the liquid is added. I use a metal tripod and bury little boards in the sand for each of its three legs to rest on.

SERVES 40

1 cup olive oil
1 small jar (8 ounces) commercially minced garlic
2 pounds chorizo, sliced
4 tablespoons pimentón
12 quarts commercial chicken stock or water
2 tablespoons salt (adjust depending on stock used)
1 gram saffron (saffron is usually sold by the gram)
1 cup Tomate Frito (page 104) or canned tomatoes
1 bag (40 ounces) frozen chicken tenders
1 bag frozen shrimp (check the count, you want 60–80 total)
1 bag (16 ounces) frozen green beans
1 jar (10 ounces) piquillo pepper strips
5 cups bomba rice
1 bag (16 ounces) frozen peas
4 pounds small clams, scrubbed and rinsed

1 You will need potholders, a large spoon or spatula to stir and serve with, as well as a knife to cut the chorizo. Everything else just gets dumped in. The liquid can be stock or water. Optional, a small gas stove and big pot to pre-heat stock.

2 Establish a good, hot bed of coals, and then heat the oil to a haze and add the garlic and give it a stir. Add the chorizo and cook until sizzling hot. Add the pimentón, chicken stock, salt, and saffron and bring to a boil. Add the Tomate Frito and the chicken, stir, and return to a boil. Stir in the shrimp, and when it returns to a boil add the beans, stir, and return to a boil. Add in the piquillo strips and rice, stirring to combine, and return to a boil. Add the peas and push the clams, hinge side down, into this burbling wet mass. Cook 20 minutes and test the rice for doneness.

3 If rice is no longer crunchy, remove from heat and let rest 10 minutes before serving. That is, if you can keep your guests at bay.

Spanish Composed Salad

The Spanish live in a climate where vegetables thrive. A visit to a market reveals stacks of ripe tomatoes and piles of greens. The standard Spanish salad is lettuce, tomatoes, and slices of sweet onion. It is accompanied with a cruet of vinegar and another of olive oil. Here is a salad that comes together quickly and easily if you just keep a few Spanish staples on hand. Plus it looks beautiful.

SERVES 6

1 head lettuce, torn into bite-size pieces
1 jar (8 ounces) white asparagus spears, drained
1 jar (13 ounces) artichoke hearts, drained
Pinch sea salt
1 tin (2 ounces) anchovies, packed in olive oil
2 tablespoons sherry vinegar
1/4 cup extra virgin olive oil
12 lemon-stuffed olives
12 caperberries or capers

1 Make a bed of lettuce on a large platter. Place asparagus spears at the center and arrange artichoke hearts around the edges. Sprinkle with the salt and arrange the anchovy fillets across the top of the salad. Sprinkle sherry vinegar over the salad and then drizzle with the olive oil. Garnish with the lemon-stuffed olives and the caperberries.

Tomatoes in Quarters

SERVES 4

4 vine-ripened tomatoes cut in quarters or eighths
1/2 teaspoon fine sea salt
1/4 cup extra virgin olive oil
1 tablespoon sherry or montilla vinegar
1 tablespoon minced parsley
1 tablespoon minced scallion, greens included
1 teaspoon minced mint leaves
1 dozen ripe black olives, such as Farga Aragon or Cuquillo or Galega

The Spanish have a tomato they pick and serve slightly green in salads, which has a hint of celery taste. I thought they were merely tomatoes that had been picked early until I saw the seed for them for sale in a garden store. But they also serve vine-ripened, mouthwatering, bright red tomatoes bursting with flavor. Use heirloom tomatoes if you can.

1 Sprinkle the tomatoes with salt and let stand. Just before serving, whisk the oil into the vinegar and then add the herbs. Pour over the tomatoes, garnish with the olives, and serve.

Salpicón (Chopped Salad with Shrimp)

SERVES 4

1 red bell pepper
1/2 English cucumber
1 yellow tomato
1 red tomato
1 pound baby shrimp meat
Pinch fine sea salt
2 tablespoons sherry wine vinegar
2 tablespoons extra virgin olive oil

In almost every tapa bar, in the display case on the counter, there is a chopped vegetable salad elaborated with seafood. The salad is deceptively simple. If ripe vegetables are used, it completely captures the purity of their flavors. This recipe uses baby shrimp, but any other seafood will work.

1 Chop the vegetables to a uniform size. Match the vegetable size to the seafood, finer for baby shrimp, larger for mussels. Toss the vegetables with the shrimp and salt to taste. Toss with the vinegar and then toss with the oil.

Jamón and Melon

SERVES 8

1 ripe melon, cantaloupe, honeydew, or other similar size melon
1/4 pound jamón serrano, thinly sliced

This is easy to prep beforehand or just wait until you get to the beach.

1 Seed the melon and then slice into eight wedges. Peel the wedges and wrap them with jamón.

VARIATION: Fry the wrapped slices in a non-stick pan until the jamón crisps, turning them once.

Piquillo Peppers Stuffed with Artichoke Salad

MAKES 18 TAPAS

1 jar (13 ounces) artichoke hearts
  from Navarra
1 small Roma tomato
1/3 cup Alioli (page 111)
1 can (10 ounces) piquillo peppers
  from Navarra

This cold version of stuffed piquillos makes an ideal tapa or salad. It requires no cooking and can be prepared in advance, if refrigerated until serving. Resting in a plastic snap-top container, the peppers transport easily.

1 Place the artichoke hearts in a colander, drain them completely and then chop. Halve the tomato; shake out the seeds, and dice, reserving only the firm flesh. It is important that there be no excess moisture in the stuffing mix. Combine the artichokes and the tomato with the Alioli.

2 Drain the piquillo peppers, then holding them point down in the circle formed with your thumb and forefinger, use a small spoon to fill them with the stuffing mixture.

Macedonia of Summer Fruits with Poppy Seed Dressing

DRESSING
1 tablespoon sherry vinegar
1/4 cup extra virgin olive oil
1 teaspoon orange blossom honey
1 tablespoon poppy seeds

The addition of poppy seeds to the dressing adds texture, flavor, and color to a fruit salad. For fruit, we suggest chunks of various colored melons, cantaloupe, honeydew, and both green and red seedless grapes cut in half. Whatever summer and the green grocer offer.

1 Whisk all ingredients to thoroughly combine.

The Iberian Picnic

The Spanish larder delivers a picnic on a whim. In Spain, we have often headed out to the local grocery market when we have found ourselves staying in some rural village. There we purchase some slices of jamón serrano, a link of hard, slicing chorizo, a chunk of Manchego cheese, and some anchovy-stuffed olives, add a loaf of bread and a bottle of chilled vino rosado and enjoy a hotel-room banquet worthy of Don Quixote.

With the rise of interest in Spanish foods, these same products can now be gathered from the shelves of a well-stocked gourmet food store at the last minute. However, if you have access to a kitchen, you can spiff up the picnic menu considerably if you have the inclination and a little foresight.

The Iberian Picnic Menu

Forage through these suggestions and pack your choices into a picnic basket.

Picnic Music from Brazil

The American jazz tenor saxophonist Stan Getz popularized the English language version of *Girl from Impanema* and other bossa nova best-sellers. His CDs remain timeless as well as those of jazz guitarist Charlie Byrd.

Bossa nova is the music most Americans associate with Brazil. But there is more. Samba is the music of Carnival and its gyrating parades. There is foro and tropicalismo, genres and sub-genres. Since his appearance singing *Cucurrucucú Paloma* in Pedro Almodóvar's movie *Talk to Her*, Caetano Veloso has gained immeasurable recognition in the United States.

Whichever you choose, the light-heartedness of the Brazilian attitude towards life will make it a perfect accompaniment to a light-hearted day outdoors.

Portuguese Lemonade or Sangría

MAKES 6 (8 OUNCE) SERVINGS

1 piri piri pepper
7 Meyer lemons, 1 of them sliced
1 cup orange blossom honey
2 tablespoons minced cilantro
1 liter carbonated soda

Let's face it, if you are on a picnic, you probably drove to the park and you are going to need to drive home. You most likely have invited the kids to come along, and the dog, and he brought his Frisbee. So you might want to serve something non-alcoholic.

1 Place the pepper in a 1½ liter pitcher and crush with a pestle. Juice 6 of the lemons and pour the juice into the pitcher. Warm the honey in a microwave and add to the juice, stirring well. Add the cilantro and the lemon slices. Just before serving, add soda and taste.

If Meyer lemons are not available, you may want to add sweetener.

FOR ADULTS: If you are not driving, turn this into a refreshing sangría by substituting a bottle Vinho Verde for 750 milliliters of the carbonated soda (use a 12-ounce container).

The Spanish Table Classic Red Gazpacho

SERVES 6 TO 8

2 to 3 cloves garlic, peeled
1 teaspoon salt
½ sweet onion, optional
1 red bell pepper
1 green bell pepper, optional
1 cucumber, peeled
4 to 5 ripe tomatoes
¼ cup sherry vinegar
¼ cup extra virgin olive oil
2 cups stale bread cubes
Salt, to taste

A jug with a secure lid filled with chilled, seasonal soup is the first thing to slip into your picnic basket. Gazpacho is one of those dishes that depend on the cook's taste buds because from batch to batch, the flavors of the ingredients vary. But no matter who makes it, gazpacho is always refreshing, and the variations lend personality. So add or subtract ingredients at whim with one caveat: it is the bread and oil that distinguishes gazpacho from vegetable juice. All measurements approximate as size, ripeness, and flavor of ingredients varies seasonally.

1 Drop garlic into a blender while running, then add ingredients one by one and purée. Add cold water if needed to allow the machine to properly blend ingredients. As the blender fills, dump half the contents into bowl or pitcher, watching for lumps. Stir and taste. If needed, adjust the salt. If too sweet, add vinegar. Add a pinch of sugar if too acidic. Add bread if too thin. Add water if too thick. Chill before serving.

Yellow Gazpacho

SERVES 4

2 large yellow bell peppers, roughly chopped

1 pound ripe yellow tomatoes, cut into wedges, excess seeds shaken out

1 (1 pound) cucumber, peeled and any large seeds removed, roughly chopped

1/2 cup stale bread chunks

1/2 cup extra virgin olive oil

1 tablespoon mild sherry vinegar

1 teaspoon sea salt

1/4 teaspoon ground cumin seeds

1/2 teaspoon sugar

6 tablespoon minced cilantro leaves

If enough are available, I always recommend using a single variety of heirloom tomato in gazpacho for the varietal experience if nothing more. I think you will also be delighted to discover the subtle variations in flavor. In Huelva, in Andalucía near the Portuguese border, they add often cumin and cilantro to gazpacho, which is exactly what I have done here.

1 Place all of the ingredients except cilantro in a blender and purée. Taste and adjust the acidity by either adding vinegar or a pinch of sugar. Chill.

2 Before serving, taste again, and then adjust to taste for salt and cumin. Garnish with the cilantro.

3 If you want to serve 6, add 1/2 pound yellow tomatoes and 1/2 cup bread chunks.

Ripe Melon Soup with Jamón

SERVES 4–6

1 ripe melon, seeded and peeled, (cantaloupe, honeydew or other similar size melon)

2 tablespoons key lime juice

4 ounces lean jamón cut into 24 matchsticks

This recipe is inspired by Andalucía's Moorish heritage.

1 Purée the melon in a food processor, adding the lime juice, adjusting to taste, and chill. When serving, stack the jamón sticks on top in little pyramids as gracefully as your dexterity allows.

Piquillo and Hummus Salad

MAKES 10 TAPAS

1/4 teaspoon sweet pimentón

1/2 pint hummus (a commercial tub from the grocery store is fine)

1 jar (7.5 ounces) whole piquillo peppers

1 teaspoon balsamic-process Rioja wine vinegar

1 tablespoon extra virgin olive oil

1 teaspoon shredded mint leaves

You want to eat well on a picnic but, in summertime in particular, you would rather not be a slave to a hot stove. Here the piquillo meets North Africa, which is visible from Tarifa and Algeciras and was, of course, under Spanish influence during their colonial era in Morocco. Spain still retains the enclaves of Ceuta and Melilla.

1 Stir the pimentón into the hummus and use it to fill the piquillos. Whisk the vinegar and oil together, then add the mint. Use this vinaigrette to dress the piquillos.

Marinated Manchego

SERVES 6

1 sprig fresh thyme, or $1/2$
  teaspoon dry
1 sprig fresh rosemary, or $1/2$
  teaspoon dry
$1/4$ teaspoon cumin seeds
12 arbequina olives
1 pound Manchego, cut into wedges
  then cut into slices
1 cup extra virgin arbequina olive
  oil

Arbequina olives produce a wonderful olive oil and have lots of flavor. I use an old fashioned clamp-top canning jar for this recipe, but any jar works.

1 Put the sprigs of thyme and rosemary in the bottom of a jar with the cumin seeds and the olives. Fill the jar with triangular slices of Manchego cheese stacked in a spiral, then top off with the olive oil. Allow to marinate for at least a week in your refrigerator. When you are ready to serve, bring to room temperature and take out as many slices as you need. If you eat all the olives, but not all the cheese, add more olives and put the jar back in the refrigerator for another day. Be sure the olive oil covers the entire surface.

Sharon's Spanglished Potato Salad

SERVES 6

3 cups cubed potatoes, boiled
1 tablespoon minced sweet onion
$1/2$ teaspoon finely ground Spanish
  sea salt
1 teaspoon Dijon mustard
$1/2$ teaspoon sweet smoked
  pimentón
$3/4$ cup Alioli (page 111)
$1/2$ cup piquillo pepper strips,
  roughly chopped
6 caperberries, sliced, for garnish,
  optional
Pinch salt

Potato salad is almost always served in tapa bars. For the most part it tastes exactly like potato salad. My wife, Sharon, had always made potato salad just like her mother made it, which is to say, according to Betty Crocker. But one day Sharon and I were headed to a party where The Spanish Table's reputation for producing Spanish-flavored foods would be at stake, so she spanglished her mother's potato salad recipe by substituting Alioli for mayo, pimentón for black pepper, and by adding piquillo pepper strips. In a dire emergency, you can actually gussy up store-bought potato salad by mixing in the pinch of pimentón and chopped piquillo peppers or add hard-boiled eggs.

1 Mix all ingredients. Taste and adjust ingredients to your personal preference.

Poached Turkey Breast Sandwich

SERVES 6

1 boneless, skinless turkey breast
4 cloves garlic, left whole with
  skin on
1 bay leaf
1 cup olive oil

Almost every turkey roasted in a home in the United States is roasted on Thanksgiving Day. In order to extend their season, turkey ranchers have come up with some innovative products such as boneless breasts and ground turkey. The problem for me has been that the cooked meat often turns out dry. So I tried poaching a deboned turkey breast in olive oil. The results were moist and tender.

1 Push down on the breast with the heel of your hand to flatten it to a uniform depth. Place it in the smallest cazuela it fits into with the garlic cloves and bay leaf. Fill with olive oil until almost covered, remembering that as the oil heats, it expands. Cook slowly until the meat is cooked through; drain and cool, then thinly slice.

2 Serve with Extra Virgin Olive Oil Mayonesa (page 110) flavored with a pinch of pimentón and crisp lettuce on crusty bread.

Peaches Poached in Moscatel Wine

SERVES 6

6 ripe peaches
1 cup sweet Moscatel wine
Orange blossom honey, optional
12 hazelnuts, crushed with a
  pestle in a mortar

Summer brings succulent peaches. These can be made in advance and transported to the picnic in a container with a secure lid. For added flippancy, slip a can of pressurized whipping cream into your cooler.

1 Place the whole peaches in a covered saucepan or olla with the wine. Bring to a boil, reduce heat, and simmer until they are soft and slump slightly.

2 This can also be done in a 350 degree F oven. Remove the peaches from the pan, reserving the juice and the peels, which will fall away from the fruit with only a gentle prodding.

3 Turn up the heat and quickly reduce the pan juices to a sugar syrup. If the peaches were ripe, no additional sweetener will be needed. If not, add a tablespoon of orange blossom honey. Strain and serve over peaches, garnishing with the hazelnuts.

Spanish Market Week Tapa Party

Spanish Market is a festive time in Santa Fe with all the streets closed so that vendors can set up their stands. It also coincides with the annual ten day International Flamenco Workshop. The workshop offers classes conducted by both local flamenco performers and guest instructors from Spain for children and adults. With everyone in town, and the restaurants jam-packed, we invite our friends over for a tapa party.

Tapas

Tapas are great for parties and gatherings large or small. Here are some ideas that have worked for events at The Spanish Table. One of the things you need to decide when planning your menu is how the tapas will be served. As finger food? With plates? With plates and forks? Will the guests be standing or seated? If the tapa needs to be cut with a knife, guests who are standing will find themselves doing contortions.

Folk Music with Tapas

Both Basque and Sephardic music speaks of days long gone by, reaching back across the years to the sounds of ancient instruments and songs sung in old stone halls. Kepa Junkera is the best known of the contemporary Basque accordion players and has recorded with many well-known guest artists, from Portugal's Dulce Pontes to Ireland's Chieftains. His group has toured the United States where he played mostly to audiences populated by persons of Basque heritage, but his music is accessible to all.

Sephardic music has been recorded by several artists and performers. In Santa Fe, Conseulo Luz has recorded a Sephardic album.

Montaditos (Mini Open-Faced Sandwiches)

Montaditos, little "mounted" tapas, are a morsel of food riding atop a small slice of bread moistened with a spread and then garnished. The layers can be simple or complex. If the structure is very vertical, a toothpick is inserted to stabilize it. Your imagination should be your guide in creating these tapas. For seafood montaditos, spread some alioli or romesco on a slice of chewy bread and top with baby shrimp meat, a single prawn, or a chunk of bonito tuna. For a vegetarian alternative, use a quarter of an artichoke heart or a section of a white asparagus spear. A slice of hard-boiled egg can be added as a layer for a more complex montadito.

THE BASE
1 For the base, slice a baguette bread loaf into thin slices. The flavor of some montaditos can be enriched by frying the bread slices in olive oil. Alternatively, toast the slices under a broiler. Crackers can sometimes be substituted.

SPREADS
2 While spreads can be as simple as a brush of mayonnaise or Alioli, plain or flavored with saffron, capers, anchovy paste, or pimentón. To the right are some more complex spreads that really need no more than a parsley leaf as garnish.

A TAPAS PARTY

We fell in love with tapas the first time we visited Spain. The thought that you could step into a bar and order a caña of beer or a copita of wine, and while sipping could sample a half dozen uniquely flavored dishes was our idea of heaven.

Tapas have become a bit of a fad in the United States. However, in 1985, the year of our first trip to Spain, tapas were pretty much an unknown. We returned from our trip crazy about tapas, and we wanted to share our enthusiasm. The guest list for our annual holiday party was expanded to include almost everyone we knew just so we could have an excuse to prepare dozens of different tapas. We planned for weeks; we cooked for two days.

By the afternoon of our party, the refrigerator was completely packed. We extended our dining room table to its full size and covered it with all the different dishes. By the time the first guests arrived, our dining room looked just like a tapa bar in Spain.

I am sure many people came out of culinary curiosity. There were no Spanish restaurants in Seattle in those days, so our party was the first place our friends could experience Spanish food. At first, many of them wondered aloud what had inspired two Seattle natives to host a party featuring the food and wine of Spain. But as they tasted the tapas and other treats, they knew why.

Piquillo-Romesco Spread

This spread marries essential Spanish flavors: sun-drenched peppers and almonds.

MAKES 1¹/₂ CUPS

¹/₄ cup Spanish Marcona almonds
¹/₄ cup olive oil
1 teaspoon minced garlic
¹/₂ teaspoon pimentón, sweet or hot, to taste
Pinch sea salt
1 can (10 ounces) piquillo peppers
    1 tablespoon extra virgin olive oil

1 Fry the almonds in olive oil until golden; set aside while they cool. Blend the remaining ingredients with a mortar and pestle or in a food processor until a slightly lumpy paste is formed. Adjust thickness by adding a splash of extra virgin olive oil.

Aceituna-Tuna Spread

Aceitunas are olives. Olivada is a simple purée of olives and olive oil. Serve this spread as a montadito on a slice of fried bread.

SERVES 16

1 (7 ounce) can tuna packed in olive oil
1 tablespoon minced onion
4 teaspoons mayonnaise
2 piquillo peppers
¹/₄ cup Olivada (page 110)
1 teaspoon capers
Salt
16 slices bread, fried in olive oil
1 egg, hard-boiled
2 tablespoons finely minced parsley

1 Drain the tuna and place in a mortar and work in the onion, mayonnaise, peppers, Olivada, capers, and salt with a pestle, or put into a food processor and pulse until well blended. Coat the bread slices with the mixture.

2 Sieve the boiled egg over the top. To sieve the egg, press it through the wire mesh with the back of a spoon. Sprinkle parsley over the tops.

Artichoke Heart and Manchego Cheese Spread

The artichoke hearts of Navarra are the world's most tender, and Manchego, the sheep cheese of La Mancha, is Spain's most popular.

MAKES 1¹/₂ CUPS

1 teaspoon chopped garlic
¹/₄ cup extra virgin olive oil
1 jar (24 ounces) artichoke hearts from Navarra
2 tablespoons lemon juice
¹/₂ cup grated Manchego
¹/₄ cup minced parsley

1 Sauté the garlic in the oil until soft, and then put all of the ingredients in a food processor and process until blended.

Marinated Vegetables

There are a great many tapas you can make in advance, such as marinated vegetables, because they are packed in vinegar. If you are making several vegetables, plunge each into their own individual marinade by varying the herbs and the type of vinegar, cava, wine, or sherry, to lend each with its own unique flavor variant. Some vegetables benefit from blanching prior to marinating. Have fun experimenting.

SOME IDEAS FOR VEGETABLES TO MARINATE

Pearl onions
Mushroom caps
Artichoke hearts
Carrots
Green beans
Asparagus spears
Eggplant
Cauliflower

BASIC MARINADE
1/4 cup Spanish vinegar, either wine vinegar, cava vinegar, sherry vinegar, or PX vinegar
Pinch Spanish sea salt
Pinch one or more of the herbs and flavorings listed at right

1 Cut the vegetables into bite-size pieces and place in a container with a tight-fitting lid. Add vinegar, salt, and herbs. Refrigerate 24 hours, turning over occasionally to evenly distribute marinade.

2 Some ideas for herbs and flavorings:

- Pebrella
- Thyme
- Oregano
- Rosemary
- Cumin
- Coriander
- Bay leaf
- Saffron

- Parsley
- Cilantro
- Garlic
- Citrus zest
- Membrillo
- Pimentón
- Piri piri

Piquillo Peppers Stuffed with Tuna Salad

These quick and easy stuffed peppers make fun tapas.

MAKES 18 SALADS OR TAPAS

STUFFING
1 can (7 ounces) bonito tuna packed in olive oil, drained
2 tablespoons chopped green olives and/or caperberries
1/2 teaspoon sherry vinegar
1/3 cup mayonnaise

1 can (10 ounces) piquillo peppers from Navarra

1 Mix all the stuffing ingredients.

2 Drain the piquillo peppers, then, holding them point down in the circle formed with your thumb and forefinger, use a small spoon to fill them with the stuffing mixture.

VARIATIONS For extra depth, use anchovy-filled olives. For a touch of sunshine, use lemon-stuffed olives.

Coca (Catalan Pizza)

SERVES 4

1 unbaked pizza crust
Olive oil or Sofrito (page 104) or
    Pisto (page 107)

TOPPINGS
Black olives
Artichoke hearts
Piquillo peppers
Morrón peppers
White asparagus spears
Anchovies
Butifarra sausage

The first time we went to Barcelona, we noticed in all the windows of bakeries what looked like cookie sheets filled with pizza. An inquiry taught us that this was coca, Catalan pizza. A crust is rolled out into a rectangular shape and covered with a topping. Coca is prepared in both a sweet version with honey and pine nuts and many savory versions. It seldom, if ever, includes cheese. The sauces and toppings play down tomato, thus distinguishing its flavor from pizza.

1 Preheat oven to 450 degrees F.

2 To make coca, use your favorite pizza crust recipe and roll the dough into a rectangular shape that fills a cookie sheet.

3 Brush the crust with olive oil or spread on some Sofrito, a sauce incorporating more red pepper than tomato, or some Pisto.

4 Then sparingly adorn it with your choice of toppings. But no cheese. Well, maybe just a smidgen of fresh goat cheese.

5 Bake 15 minutes until the crust browns and the sauce bubbles.

6 Coca is a light and refreshing snack. Since it starts out as a rectangle, it can be cut it into easy-to-handle squares that can be served as finger food at your tapa party.

Sardine Pâté

SERVES 2–4

1 tin Portuguese sardines packed
    in olive oil
2 tablespoons minced cilantro
1 Key lime, juiced
$1/4$ cup mayonnaise, optional
Pinch salt, to taste

When you sit down in a Portuguese restaurant, they bring a basket of bread rolls along with a little cheese and some fish pâté made from tuna or sardines. If you eat them, they show up on your bill. They cost next to nothing and as I am Captain Curious when it comes to little tastes of things, I sample them all.

1 Empty the tin of sardines with the oil into a large yellow mortar and crush with a pestle. Add the cilantro and lime juice and push into mixture with pestle. You now have a rough fish pâté. If softening with mayonnaise, add it now and work it in. Taste and add salt. Serve with bread or crisp crackers.

Baby Turkey Meatballs

MAKES 36 SMALL MEATBALLS

1 cup Picada (page 108)
1 pound ground turkey meat
1/4 cup flour
1/4 cup olive oil

GRAVY
1 tablespoon minced garlic
2 tablespoons olive oil, if needed
2 tablespoons flour
1/2 cup Madeira

It is more traditional to use ground pork or lamb (or a combination of ground meats, including veal or beef), but the use of turkey puts a new twist on the tradition.

1 Knead the Picada into the meat, mixing well. If prepping in advance, you can refrigerate this mixture overnight.

2 Form into little balls by rolling between your hands. At this point, you can lay them out in a single layer and hold them until just before the party. Or, you can lay them out on baking sheets and put them in the freezer until they are frozen hard. Then slip them into ziplock bags to have on hand when you need them.

3 To cook, roll the balls around in a little flour and fry them in oil in a medium cazuela. Remove while making the gravy. If you do not want to serve with a sauce, just spear the cooked meatballs with toothpicks and serve them on a platter.

GRAVY
4 Cook garlic in the same cazuela the meatballs were cooked in, adding oil if necessary. When the garlic is soft, stir in flour, one tablespoon at a time.

5 Stir in the Madeira with an olive wood spatula, deglazing the cazuela. Reduce to a thick gravy. Return meatballs to the pan and reheat in sauce before serving. Baby peas and finely diced carrots are often added to the sauce for color and texture.

VARIATION: Any of the sauces used in the following recipe for chicken drumettes can be used with meatballs.

Chicken Drumette Tapas

MAKES 20 DRUMETTES

2 tablespoons olive oil
2 pounds chicken drumettes
Pinch sea salt
1/2 to 3/4 cup sauce of choice

1 Preheat oven to 400 degrees F. Roasting chicken drumettes in a hot oven and then covering them with a sauce yields lots of great little tapas. Brush the bottom of a cazuela with olive oil and place the drumettes in it. Turn to coat with oil, sprinkle with sea salt, and bake 30 minutes, turning them once or twice. When golden brown, remove them from the cazuela and use the drippings to make a sauce. Once you are happy with the sauce, return the drumettes to the cazuela and toss to coat. Heat before serving. If you do not want chicken bones in the post-party debris, use bite-size pieces of boned chicken and spear each one with a toothpick.

Sauces

WHITE WINE SAUCE
Deglaze the cazuela with $1/2$ cup of white wine, then thicken with bread crumbs and season with some freshly grated nutmeg.

GREEN SAUCE
Add $1/4$ cup minced parsley or cilantro leaves and 1 clove garlic, minced, to the white wine sauce, omitting the nutmeg.

MOORISH SAUCE
Add 2 tablespoons Pincho Seasoning (page 106) to the white wine sauce.

RED WINE SAUCE
After cooking a tablespoon or 2 of finely diced chorizo sausage and some minced onions in the drippings, add a cup of red wine and reduce it by half.

GARLIC SAUCE
Use one head of garlic for every 24 ounces of chicken or meatballs. Slowly cook the minced garlic in meat drippings and olive oil until very soft. Whisk in 1 to 2 tablespoons flour, then $1/2$ to 1 cup white wine.

PICADA SAUCE
After deglazing the cazuela with $1/2$ cup white wine or fino sherry, add 2 tablespoons Picada (page 108).

ROMESCO SAUCE
Use Romesco (page 109) in place of picada.

SAFFRON SAUCE
Season either picada or garlic sauce with a pinch of saffron threads steeped in some sherry or white wine.

SIDRA SAUCE
Use the recipe for Catalan Chicken à la Sidra (page 86)

TOMATE FRITO
Deglaze the cazuela with a splash of Spanish brandy before adding the Tomate Frito (page 104), 1 tablespoon minced parsley, and $1/4$ teaspoon pebrella or cumin.

TIP: To make two versions of this tapa, you can roast a double quantity of the chicken drumettes and then split the pan drippings to make two sauces.

A Dessert Wine Tasting

With so many great dessert wines available from Spain and Portugal, from sherry to port to Madeira, why not have a dessert wine tasting? If you do have a tasting, and I encourage it, you will want to serve some food. The food can be something as simple as María Biscuits, the simple, sweet crackers favored all over the Hispanic world, or nuts, cheeses, and figs, or it can be an elaborate array of desserts.

A Fortified Wines Primer

Dessert Wine Tasting Music
Classic Spanish Guitar

For soothingly beautiful music to serve with your dessert wine tasting, look for music by the legendary classical guitarist, Andrés Segovia, or collections featuring the works of Spain's most famous composers of classical guitar music, Isaac Albeniz, born in Catalonia, Joaquin Rodrigo from Valencia, and Manuel de Falla from Cadiz.

A Fortified Wines Primer
Maderia, Port, and Sherry

Generally, fortified wines are made by adding alcohol (brandy) during fermentation of wine to kill the yeast before it has converted all the natural grape sugars to alcohol. This results in wines, in most cases, that are sweet and usually served after a meal. As you will see, there are many exceptions to this rule and many fortified wines that are relatively dry are served as an aperitif.

Madeiras
Rainwater

Rainwater is made from the common red grape, Tinta Negra Mole, and then artificially aged in estufa, tanks warmed with hot water or in casks exposed to solar heat. The origin of this process was the desire to replicate the effect the voyage of sailing vessels had on the shipped wines in the 1700s. At that time, some ships sailed to the American Colonies via Brazil. Casks that had been routed through the tropics commanded a premium price.

Legend has it that the name, Rainwater, and its medium-bodied style, resulted from a butt being left on a London pier where it was diluted by falling rain. More likely, a stevedore replaced his generous sample with a bucket of tap water.

Varietals

The varietals are made from the four surviving noble grapes, all white. They are listed at right from drier to sweeter. In every case, the sweetness is balanced by the sparkling acidity, which makes Madeiras different than other fortified wines. This high acidity also means that they are the most stable of all wines and keep indefinitely, even after being opened. During our visit to the wine lodges in Madeira, we tasted two-hundred-year-old Madeiras from harvests contemporary with the American Revolutionary War.

ENJOYING MADEIRA

When people choose foods to accompany a Madeira, they usually choose nuts, cheeses, or sweet biscuits. However, a dish like mushroom soup is a natural pairing. You don't really need anything to accompany a glass of vintage Madeira. Sure, a comfortable chair in a quiet room beside a fireplace with the sun slowly setting outside the window wouldn't hurt. First, glance at your watch, then close your eyes and take a tiny sip. Now wait. Enjoy the dozen flavors floating across your palate, of dried orange peel floating on butterscotch; of a eucalyptus forest brushed by a pine-scented breeze; of coffee and chocolate; of honeyed toast studded with raisins. When the last flavor evaporates from your mouth, open your eyes. Glance at your watch. Be totally amazed how much time has lapsed. Vintage Madeira has an absolutely incredible long finish.

Sercial

The driest Maderia, is grown at the highest altitude vineyards on the island.

Verdelho

Also grown in the cooler micro-climates.

Bual (Boal)

Darker, sweeter flavors layered with dried orange peel and spice.

Malmsey (Malvasia)

The sweetest, densest, and richest of the three with deep raisiny and chocolate flavors.

Aging

Supervised aging standards for Madeiras fall into three categories, which are the minimum aging for all the wine in the bottling: five years, ten years, and fifteen years.

Vintage Madeiras

Aged twenty years minimum, vintage Madeiras are one of the unique experiences available to the wine lover. Flavors range from bittersweet chocolate, burnt toast, and black tea to velvet caramel and orange peel. The residual sugars are offset by the vibrant acidity that makes Madeira unique.

Colheita Madeiras

These are "vintage" Madeiras less than twenty-five years old, a recently developed category. There are also several other new generic terms being used on Madeiras that are blends because of the European Union uniform wine labeling rules for varietals. These include terms such as Special Reserve or Full Rich.

Ports

The interest in ports has steadily increased since The Spanish Table opened. Two things seemed to be responsible. First was the cigar craze and second was a series of great vintages starting with the 1994 Vintage. A few ports are made from white wine grapes, but most are made from red wine grapes. Those can be divided into two families: tawny ports and red ports.

Ports come from grapes grown on the terraced hills leading up from the gorge of the Douro River. It is carved by the Douro as it descends from the Spanish border near Zamora to empty into the Atlantic Ocean at the city of Porto (in Spain, the same river is known as the Duero and along its banks are the respected red wine denominaciones Ribera del Duero and Toro).

Portugal, in complicity with British wine merchants, invented port. It was named after the city O Porto, "The Port" (and from the city, the name of the country: Portugal). Port is most often spelled *oporto* on a bottle of Portuguese port. It was the first regulated wine, the Denomination of Origin being established in 1756.

Tawny Ports

Tawny ports are aged in wood barrels for a minimum of seven years. During this time they lose much of their reddish color and become more caramel or tawny colored. At the same time, the winey flavors are subdued and the undertones of caramel, walnuts, and orange peel emerge into the forefront. The port lodges release a basic seven-year-old tawny as well as blends labeled ten, twenty, thirty, or forty years. The year designates the average age of the wines used in the blending.

Colheitas

They are an unblended tawny port from a specific harvest. While Colheita translates as vintage, the English word "vintage" is applied only to red ports.

Colheitas are available for many years going back as far as 1937. They reflect a specific vintage because they are actually as old as their date. For example, a Colheita from a harvest twenty years ago reflects twenty years of barrel aging in its subtle flavors, whereas a twenty-year-old blend is an average of twenty years old and has some younger port in it to lend some vibrancy to its flavor profile. If you have a tawny port tasting, the difference between a blended tawny and a Colheita tawny is worth exploring. It is fun to give either a blend or Colheita to commemorate a significant birthday or anniversary.

Red Ports

Red, or ruby, ports are not barrel-aged more than a year or two, if at all. They are wine colored and have the distinct nose and flavors of sweet wine carefully balanced with tannins. Port lodges bottle a basic ruby port as well as Late Bottled Vintage ports (LBV) which are ready to drink when released. They tend to be a rich, deep purple color with moderately sweet fruit flavors of black plumb and berries. LBVs are more complex than ruby ports.

Vintage Ports

Vintage ports are the flagship wines of port lodges. They are bottled and released with great fanfare two years after the harvest. Historically, only wines from great harvests were declared and released as vintage ports, but with modern winemaking techniques and the demands of international marketing, this practice has blurred considerably. There are still declared vintage years, but single Quinta Vintage Ports are released in the intervening years.

A quinta is a farm or vineyard in Portuguese. This nomenclature in theory applies to premier vineyards with perfect soil, elevation, and exposure to sunlight. As always with wines, the proof is in the bottle, and comparison tasting, preferably blind, will let you and your compatriots decide for yourselves.

Vintage ports are released two years after the harvest. When released, they are still very young and need to be aged for up to twenty years or more before drinking. For this reason, people sometimes lay down a bottle of vintage port from a child's birth year for them to drink on their twenty-first birthday.

White Ports

These are much, much more popular in Portugal than in the United States, but they have been discovered by The Spanish Table customers.

Dry Whites

The driest of white ports are served chilled as an aperitif, sometimes with a twist of lemon zest. When aged, dry whites take on a hint of a tawny port's nuttiness and complexity.

Fine White Ports

These are medium sweet and the type you are most likely to encounter in your local wine store. The best of them taste of golden apples with a breath of butterscotch.

Lagrimas

These are the sweetest of the white ports. The term, which translates as tears, has inspired some remarkable labels over the years. Their light flavor is of honeyed walnuts.

Sherry

Sherry comes from Jerez and the nearby towns of Puerto Santa Maria and Sanlúcar. As with port, the wine was collaboratively designed with British wine merchants who wanted wines stable enough to ship in casks on sailing ships. Fortification with brandy (which is distilled wine), kept port, sherry, and Madeira from spoiling during the voyage to England and out to the Colonies. Sherries fall into a large number of categories that I have listed below, from dry to sweet.

- Fino
- Manzanilla
- Oloroso
- Amontillado
- Cortado
- Cream
- PX (Pedro Ximenex)
- Very Old Sherry
- Moscatel

Sherry starts as wine made from the palomino, a white grape. It then diverges in the barrel because of a special yeast that thrives on the climate and sea breezes unique to this coastal, river delta area.

In many barrels, a thick layer of this yeast called flor develops, forming a crust over the wine and impacting its flavor as sourdough yeasts impact the flavor of bread. If this happens, the sherry becomes fino or manzanilla with time. Manzanilla can be made only in Sanlúcar where the flor grows year round. It has the tangiest yeast flavor. Fino is made in Jerez and Puerto Santa Maria where the flor only thrives for part of the year. Fino tends to be milder flavored.

Fino and Manzanilla

These are consumed in Andalucía much as white wine is consumed elsewhere both as an aperitif and with meals. While at 15%, the alcohol in these wines is higher than in most white table wines, but it is no higher than in Zinfandel or other modern-styled red wines. They should be drunk soon after bottling while they taste the freshest. They pair well with almost any food.

Oloroso

If no flor forms on the wine, it becomes an *oloroso*, which translates as aromatic. The name arises from the wonderful nose on this wine. Oloroso sherry is made in styles ranging from dry to off dry. The label usually provides a clue.

Amontillado

When fino sherry is left in the cask after the flor forms, it oxidizes slightly, taking on a golden hue and a nutty flavor and thus becomes amontillado. Amontillados range from bone dry to slightly sweet.

Cortado

Cortados are mongrels. Before oenological science perfected sherry making, some batches emerged that were not clearly either finos or olorosos. These barrels were marked across their butt with a chalk slash, or cortado. Cortados are both aromatic and nutty flavored. They are not common but very delicious.

Cream

Cream sherries are sweetened blends. They were originally developed for English ladies to sip at tea time with their crumpets and cakes. They can be scrumptious and are perfect for sipping in front of the fire or while addressing Christmas cards or after cross-country skiing.

Pedro Ximénez, or PX

This grape is usually raisinated by being laid out on mats in the vineyards to shrivel under the blazing sun. This concentrates the grape sugars before vinification. PX is blended into cream sherries and other sherries to sweeten them. Bottled unblended, PX can be so sweet that it can be poured over ice cream as syrup. Generally speaking, PX grapes and wine originate not in Jerez, but in Montilla in Córdoba. The bodegas in Montilla make a full range of sherry-like wines such as fino and amontillado that are delicious in their own right.

Very Old Sherry

The Denomination of Origin of Jerez has long avoided both vintages and uniform aging nomenclature in favor of their solera tradition, which is depicted as a stack of barrels signifying that wines from different vintages are blended in a regulated fashion. Their goal is that every year a sherry from a given bodega should taste the same. The rules made it hard for bodegas to market, in any intelligible way, their very special, older sherries. Now they are allowed to label their thirty-year-old sherries. These are really expensive and really worth the price.

Moscatel

This grape is usually used to make sweet wines. Many sherry bodegas have plantings of moscatel in addition to palomino and make a sherry-style sweet wine from those grapes.

Other Dessert Wines

Ochoa Moscatel

This is my favorite dessert wine. Revolutionary winemaking, using temperature to stop fermentation, results in a sweet wine with low alcohol. Its nectarine and spice flavors literally dance on the palate.

El Grifo

From Lanzarote in the Canary Islands, this is another moscatel that is made using the same technique as the Ochoa due to a family tie through marriage. It has similar flavors and characteristics to the Ochoa.

Casta Diva Alicante Muscat

Made from grapes grown on ancient terraces facing the sun, the winery calls the wine Cosecha Miel, honey harvest. It is a bright dessert wine, sweet without being cloying, its nectars dance with tropical nuances.

Olivares Dulce

Made from late harvested, old vines Monastrell (a.k.a. Mouvèdre), this intense, port-like red wine has multiple dimensions that make it a treat to sip.

Málaga

Málaga is another sweet member of the sherry and montilla family. There are still some around, but many of the vineyards have been displaced by urbanization.

Moscatel de Setúbal

Setúbal is a seaside town just south of Lisbon and around it grow several varietals of muscat grapes from which this world-renowned dessert wine is made. The wine is left on the skins for several months, giving it an intense flavor.

Black Olive and Fig Tapenade

MAKES APPROXIMATELY 1¹/₂ CUPS

¹/₂ teaspoon minced garlic
¹/₈ teaspoon coarse sea salt
1 cup dried figs, chopped
¹/₂ cup Olivada (page 110)
2 tablespoons lemon juice
¹/₄ cup extra virgin olive oil
¹/₄ cup minced parsley

Spain is a land of figs and olives. Marrying them in this tapenade creates a savory-sweet spread that can be served as a tapa with wine, sherry, or port.

1 Crush the garlic and salt, and then the figs, with a mortar and pestle. Slowly add the Olivada. Thin with the lemon juice and the olive oil, then stir in parsley.

2 Or you can mix the ingredients in a food processor, pulsing until blended.

3 This is quite tasty when served as a spread with crackers or bread.

Blue Cheese and Port Montaditos with Honey-Candied Pine Nuts

MAKES 12 TAPAS

¹/₂ pound cabrales or valdeón or other Spanish blue cheese
¹/₈ cup white port
2 tablespoons extra virgin olive oil
1 apple, cored and cut into 12 slices
1 tablespoon lemon juice
12 slices raisin nut bread
¹/₄ cup olive oil
12 Saffron Syrup candied walnut halves (page 112)

The tang of the cheese and the sweetness of the nuts is a wonderful combination.

1 Using a mortar and pestle, cream the blue cheese with the port and olive oil. Dip the apple slices into lemon juice to prevent browning. Fry the bread slices in the oil, and then spread a little of the cheese on each piece of bread. Top with a slice of apple and a candied walnut.

Olive Oil Toast with Chocolate

MAKES 6 TAPAS

6 slices baguette
¹/₄ cup olive oil
6 pieces Spanish dark chocolate
3 teaspoons extra virgin olive oil

One night in Barcelona we went to a trendy new tapa bar where Sharon ordered this dessert. Since it was an open kitchen, we could watch it being prepared, not that there is really any mystery to it. As soon as she got home, she re-created it and has served it several times since to company.

1 Fry the baguette slices in the oil. Place one piece of chocolate on each bread slice and run them under the broiler until melted. Drizzle with extra virgin olive oil.

Chocolate Port Wine Cake

Red port and chocolate are old friends and they mingle in this intensely rich chocolate cake.

SERVES 10

5 ounces unsalted butter
6 ounces bittersweet chocolate, chopped
2/3 cup Ruby or LBV port
4 ounces blanched Marcona almonds
3/4 cup plus 1 tablespoon sugar, divided
4 large eggs, separated, at room temperature
1 cup flour
Pinch salt

FROSTING
1 cup whipping cream
8 ounces bittersweet chocolate

1 Preheat oven to 350 degrees F.

2 Warm the butter, chocolate, and port in a double boiler until melted, then set aside to cool to lukewarm.

3 Place the almonds and 1 tablespoon sugar in a food processor, pulsing to grind into a powder. The sugar will help prevent the almonds from turning into nut butter. Whip the egg yolks and ½ cup of the sugar with an electric beater on high for 3 minutes until slightly increased in volume.

4 Reduce the beater speed to low and incorporate the chocolate mixture. Combine flour and salt, add to mixture, and beat until well blended.

5 Clean and dry the beaters and whip the egg whites with the remaining ¼ cup of sugar until they peak. (If the beaters are not dry, the eggs may not peak properly.) Gently fold half the egg whites into the chocolate-egg yolk batter, then repeat with the other half. Mix until just incorporated.

6 Bake in a 9 x 9-inch cake pan lined with parchment paper for approximately 35 minutes or until the cake pulls away from the sides of the pan and springs back from a touch.

7 Cover the top with bittersweet chocolate frosting.

FROSTING
8 Bring the cream to a boil and whisk in the chocolate. Cool to room temperature before frosting the cake.

Citrus Trio

Since Spain is far enough south to be within sight of North Africa, it has warm microclimates. It is blessed with fruits from temperate to tropical, from apples to mangos. The Spanish love fruit and it is always an appropriate dessert.

SERVES 4

¼ cup lemon or lime juice
2 tablespoons membrillo
4 oranges
1 grapefruit
¼ pound Manchego

1 Whisk the lemon juice into the membrillo until it reaches the consistency of heavy cream.

2 Peel the oranges and grapefruit with a knife, removing the white pith, and then slice. Place slices on individual plates and pour the lemon sauce over the fruit. Using a vegetable peeler, shave curls of the Manchego over the top.

The Holiday Feasts

In Spain, Christmas is more about feasts than gifts. Those gifts that do arrive are brought by the three kings at the end of the Christmas season on the day of Epiphany. Christmas Eve features a dinner with a traditional menu. After dinner, at midnight, there is the *Misa de Gallo*, with the church filled with the light of hundreds of candles. Christmas Day is shared with all the relatives who are able to gather together to celebrate with food and drink.

On the following pages are some specific suggestions for holiday menus, but don't neglect to consult the other chapters.

Paella has become a huge holiday favorite of my customers, served on Christmas Eve or the day after Thanksgiving using turkey stock made from the carcass and including some scraps of leftover turkey meat.

Holiday Music
Villancicos

No holiday is as closely linked to music as Christmas. The tradition in Spain is to sing Villancicos, folksongs dating back to the fifteenth century. Some examples include *El Niño Del Carpintero*, *A Belén Pastores*, *Ha Nacido El Niño*, *Campana Sobre Campana*, and *Los Peces en El Río*.

Blood Orange and Cranberry Sangría

SERVES 4

1 cup water
1/2 cup sugar
1 pound whole cranberries
3 blood oranges, sliced
1 bottle (750 milliliters) white wine, chilled
1 can (12 ounces) lemon-lime soda, chilled

Blood oranges arrive in the markets along with winter weather. Their juice is often so red that when we encountered it sold on the streets of southern Europe on our travels, we thought it was tomato juice.

1 Put the water, sugar, and cranberries in a small saucepan and bring to a boil. Remove from heat and let cool. Then pour into a pitcher with 1 1/2 liter capacity. Add the orange slices and muddle gently with a wooden pestle to release juices. Add the wine and soda and serve over ice cubes.

Clementine Orange Salad

SERVES 6

1 tablespoon PX sherry vinegar
1 teaspoon Saffron Syrup (page 162), or orange blossom honey
2 tablespoons extra virgin olive oil
8 Spanish clementine oranges, peeled and segmented
2 tablespoons sliced almonds, toasted

Boxes of little clementine oranges from Spain appear in our markets around Thanksgiving. They are easy to peel, and after the segments are dressed with a drizzle of saffron syrup and topped with toasted almond slices, they can be served as a festive salad or as a dessert, the sweetness adjusted accordingly.

1 Combine the first 3 ingredients and gently toss with the oranges. Then top with almond slices and serve.

Winter Macedonia of Fresh Fruit

SERVES 6

2 firm winter pears, 1 green, 1 red
2 oranges, preferably Spanish clementines
1/2 pomegranate
2 tablespoons quince membrillo
1 lime
1 tablespoon pine nuts, toasted

Here is another salad of fruits available in the midst of winter. In Spanish, pomegranate is *granada*, from Arabic.

1 Core and cut the pears into chunks. Remove skin from the oranges, slice crosswise, and separate into segments, saving the small amount of juice that collects from the preparation. Separate the seeds from the pomegranate and combine with the pears and oranges.

2 Use the orange juice to dilute the membrillo, adding a squeeze of lime juice to taste. Toss with fruit and sprinkle pine nuts on top.

Turkey with Catalan Stuffing

1 turkey, size depends upon
   number of people being served

BASTING MIXTURE
2 tablespoons coarse sea salt
$^1/_2$ teaspoon saffron threads
8 cloves garlic, minced
$^1/_2$ cup olive oil
1 large orange, quartered
1 lemon, quartered
$^1/_2$ cup amontillado sherry

STUFFING
SERVES 8
1 cup raisins
2 cups chopped onions
2 tablespoons olive oil
1 cup Spanish pine nuts
1 bunch spinach, chopped
4 cups cubed stale bread

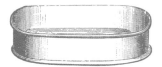

Introduce a touch of Barcelona to your traditional Thanksgiving dinner with this Iberian take on roast turkey.

1 Preheat oven to 450 degrees F.

2 Clean and prepare the turkey for cooking.

3 Place the salt and saffron in a mortar and use a pestle to grind them together. Add the garlic, mash to paste, and slowly add the oil. Using a pastry brush, paint the turkey with this mixture. Quarter the orange and lemon, and slip them into the bird's cavity. Place the turkey in a very large cazuela and pour the sherry over it.

4 Roast, basting every 20 to 30 minutes using the juices collected in the bottom of the cazuela. When done, remove the turkey from the pan and set it aside to rest.

5 While the turkey is resting, pour off the drippings and separate the fat from the juices, reserving some fat if you intend to make gravy. De-

glaze the roasting pan with $^1/_2$ cup of water, then add it to the juices.

6 Turn oven temperature down to 350 degrees F.

7 To make the stuffing, place the raisins in a bowl and cover with some of the turkey juice to re-hydrate.

8 Sauté the onions with the oil in the deglazed cazuela. Toss with the other stuffing ingredients in a large mixing bowl. Add enough of the juices from roasting pan to dampen the stuffing. Any extra juice can be used if you make gravy. Put stuffing in a cazuela and bake until heated through and surface is crisp, approximately 30 minutes.

9 After turkey has rested, carve and serve with stuffing.

ROASTING CHESTNUTS

Roasting chestnuts on an open fire is a seasonal delight. The same factory that makes our paella pans makes chestnut roasting pans. Shaped like frying pans, these have holes the size of nickels all over the bottom. They come in two versions, one with a normal handle for using over a gas range or barbecue, and the other with a 28-inch handle so you can stay back from the heat of a roaring bonfire while you occasionally shake the pan. You know the chestnuts are ready when the skins split. A glass of tawny port makes a great accompaniment.

Chestnut and Cardoon Soup

SERVES 4–6

SERVES 4–6

1 jar (7 ounces, about 24 nuts)
  Spanish chestnuts
1 jar (14 ounces) cooked cardoons
2 cups chicken stock
2 tablespoons Spanish extra virgin
  olive oil

1 In a food processor, grind the chestnuts to a rough powder. Add the cardoons and purée.

2 Heat the chicken stock in an olla to boiling and stir in the chestnut mixture. Reduce the heat and cook 1 or 2 minutes to meld flavors.

3 Add a swirl of olive oil to each bowl while serving.

Chestnut and Chorizo Fideuá

SERVES 4

4 Spanish cooking chorizo (or
  linguiça)
1/2 pound fideo noodles
1 jar (24 nuts) Spanish chestnuts,
  sliced (they will tend to crumble)
2 quarts chicken or turkey stock,
  defatted

Chestnuts are harvested late in the year. There would also be chorizo then, from the fall *matanza*, pig butchering, which requires cool weather. Inevitably, they end up in the same dish, here with fideo pasta.

1 Slowly heat the chorizo in a 12-inch or larger paella pan until it releases some fat, then increase the heat and brown the sausage. When the chorizo is crisped, add the pasta and cook until the noodles are toasted, stirring once or twice. Stir in the chestnuts and add the stock and bring to a boil.

2 Simmer 11–15 minutes until the stock is absorbed and the pasta is cooked.

Cardoon Gratin

SERVES 4

1 jar (14 ounces) cardoons,
  drained
1 cup heavy cream or half-and-half
1/4 cup grated San Simon or
  Idiazabal cheese
1/4 cup Pimentón Bread Crumbs
  (page 122)

Cardoons are a popular dish in Navarra, where they are traditionally served on Christmas Eve. The Basque cheese in this recipe adds just a hint of smoke.

1 Preheat oven to 350 degrees F.

2 Divide the cardoons between four small cazuelas. Fill the cazuelas halfway with cream. Sprinkle with the cheese and then the bread crumbs. Bake until browned and bubbly, about 15 minutes.

Christmas Mussels

These mussels feel like Christmas because the vinaigrette is flecked with bits of red and green vegetables. They are simple and can be prepared in advance. The result is colorful.

EACH MUSSEL IS A PORTION

Buy as many as you need. The following ingredients are enough for 2 pounds of mussels.

MARINADE
1 tablespoon very finely diced sweet onion
1 tablespoon very finely diced red bell pepper
1 tablespoon very finely diced green bell pepper
1 tablespoon small capers
$^1/_4$ cup extra virgin olive oil
$^1/_4$ cup white wine vinegar

1 Prepare the mussels by steaming them briefly until they open. Then remove the meat from the shells. Throw away half of the shells. Rinse the other half and put them in a bag in the refrigerator.

2 Put the mussel meat in a jar with a tight-fitting lid and add the marinade ingredients. Shake to coat and refrigerate 24 hours. If you think of it, give it a shake during this period to keep everything distributed nicely.

3 When it is time to serve, place a mussel in each shell and spoon some of the marinade and diced vegetables over them. Serve them on a chilled platter. If it is to be a long party, place the platter on a bed of ice.

Spanish Sauce for Christmas Ham

This red wine and raisin sauce complements the richness of the meat and elevates it to a special-occasion dish.

MAKES APPROXIMATELY 1 CUP

$^1/_4$ cup yellow raisins
8 pitted prunes
1 cup red wine
1 orange, zest and juice
$^1/_4$ teaspoon nutmeg
$^1/_4$ teaspoon ground clove
2 tablespoons cornstarch
2 tablespoons Spanish brandy
$1^1/_2$ teaspoons Saffron Candied Lemon Zest (page 113)

1 Chop the raisins and the prunes and steep in the red wine 30 minutes until the fruits are plumped.

2 Drain and deglaze the ham roasting pan using the wine from the fruit.

3 Add the raisins, prunes, orange juice, zest, nutmeg, and cloves. Bring to a boil and reduce by half. Mix the cornstarch with the brandy and whisk the resulting paste into the pan until fully incorporated. Add the candied lemon zest. Cook until it thickens into a light gravy.

Migas with Pumpkin and Brandy

SERVES 8

Pinch saffron
2 tablespoons Spanish brandy
1 cup chicken stock
¹/₄ cup olive oil
1 pound pumpkin or squash meat, cubed
¹/₄ cup diced jamón trimmings, the fattier the better
¹/₄ cup diced chorizo
1 onion, chopped
4 cups cubed stale bread

In Salamanca, they sometimes slip a little pumpkin into the migas. Adding either pumpkin or squash cubes makes this a seasonal and festive dish.

1 Preheat oven to 350 degrees F.

2 Place the saffron in a medium saucepan with the brandy and heat just to a boil. Add the chicken stock and let simmer until it is needed.

3 Heat the oil in a 10-inch cazuela con tapa. Sauté the pumpkin cubes slowly until they soften or, alternatively, put them in the microwave and cook for a couple of minutes until they pierce easily with a fork but are still firm. Add the jamón to the cazuela and cook until the fat is rendered, and then add the chorizo. When chorizo is sizzling hot, add the onion and cook until translucent. Add the bread cubes and toss to distribute the ingredients evenly. Press the bread down to form an even surface. Pour the hot saffron stock over the bread mix.

4 Cover (if using a regular cazuela without a top, cover with foil) and bake in the oven for 10 minutes. Remove and bake uncovered an additional 10 minutes.

Saffron Baked Apples

SERVES 6

6 firm apples, cored but peel left on
6 tablespoons butter, divided
6 tablespoons Saffron Syrup (page 112)
¹/₂ cup sweet Madeira (Rainwater or Malmsey, depending on your budget)
1 cup Saffron-Scented Whipped Cream (page 142)

This is Spanish-style baked apples.

1 Preheat oven to 350 degrees F.

2 Place the cored apples upright in a large olla. Put 1 tablespoon of butter in the center of each apple. Drizzle with Saffron Syrup and add Madeira.

3 Bake 40 minutes.

4 Remove apples to a warmed serving dish. Reduce the leftover liquid in the olla at a high heat until it forms a thick sauce. Pour over apples and top with whipped cream, if desired. Serve while still warm.

Galician Rustic Raisin Bread

MAKES A 2¹/₂ POUND LOAF OF MEDIUM-DENSE BREAD

SPONGE
1 package dry yeast
¹/₂ cup warm water
¹/₂ cup unbleached flour
1 tablespoon chestnut honey

DOUGH
1 cup raisins
¹/₂ cup tawny port
¹/₂ cup chestnut honey
1 cup chopped walnuts
1 teaspoon salt
¹/₈ cup extra virgin olive oil
¹/₂ cup beer, at room temperature
¹/₂ cup milk, at room temperature
4 cups unbleached flour, divided
Cornmeal

This is not a sweet bread, just a humble bread that has been dressed up for a special occasion.

SPONGE

1 In a large, warm bowl, combine the sponge ingredients, stirring to form a batter. Cover and let proof in a warm, but not hot, place until the surface is broken by myriad bubbles and the batter has turned into a light and spongy mass. This should take 30 minutes, and you should have about twice the mass you started with.

DOUGH

2 While the sponge is proofing, soak the raisins in the port to re-hydrate them. When the sponge is ready, add all the other ingredients to it except the flour. Now stir in 3 cups flour, ¹/₂ cup at a time. By the time you are done, you should have a stiff but finger-friendly dough. Turn it out onto a floured board and knead 5 to 10 minutes until you feel it become elastic. It will be sticky, so keep dusting your hands and the dough with the reserved cup of flour as needed. Shape it into a ball.

3 Pour a little olive oil in a large bowl and put the ball of dough in the bowl and turn it over, oiled side up. Cover and let rise until doubled in bulk, about an hour.

4 Turn the ball out, punch down, knead another 5 minutes, dusting again with reserved flour, then return it to the re-oiled bowl for a second rise.

5 When it has redoubled in bulk, punch down and knead another 5 minutes and form it into any shaped loaf you like and cover with waxed paper to keep it cozy and warm.

6 While the dough is rising for the third time, preheat the oven to 500 degrees F. If you use a baking stone, place it on the center rack. Place a pan in the bottom of the oven for the water.

7 When risen, place the loaf on a baking sheet dusted with corn-meal to prevent sticking. Now you can slash the top if, when baking, you are a slasher like me. Slide it in the oven and carefully add water to the hot pan to make lots of steam. Bake 15 minutes.

8 Reduce the heat to 400 degrees F and add more water to the pan. Bake another 25 minutes until the crust is dark brown and it sounds hollow when you knock on it.

Turrón and Chocolate Bread Pudding

SERVES 10

1/2 cup cream sherry
1/2 cup raisins
1 (7 ounce) bar turrón blando (jijona)
1 (6 ounce) bar 70% cocoa chocolate
2 cups milk
1 tablespoon vanilla extract
Zest of 1 orange, candied in Saffron Syrup (page 113) and finely diced
1/4 teaspoon fine sea salt
5 eggs
8 cups cubed stale bread (leftover holiday sweet breads work great)

A customer once confided in me that the day after Three Kings Day, any turrón left in her house goes to the Food Bank. "In self defense," she said. Here is an alternative, turn it into a dessert for, say, Presidents Day weekend when everyone has recovered from their holiday gluttony. But this is also a great Christmas Day dessert using the leftovers from the Christmas Eve dessert buffet.

1 Pour the sherry over the raisins and set aside.

2 Chop up the turrón bar and the chocolate. Heat the milk to scalding (I use the microwave) and pour over the chopped candies. Stir to dissolve. Add the raisins, vanilla, candied orange zest, and salt. Beat the eggs and whisk them into the mix. Pour over the bread cubes and let sit 1 hour while bread absorbs moisture.

3 Preheat oven to 350 degrees F.

4 Place the mix in a 10-inch cazuela or in individual 4-inch cazuelas and bake pudding until it browns on top. It should be firm but still wiggly. This will take 30–45 minutes depending on your oven and which pan size you elect to use.

TURRÓN

Turrón, which dates back to the Moors, is made of almonds and honey. In its highest form, the almonds are Marcona almonds and the honey is orange blossom honey. The higher the percentage of almonds, which can range from 50 to 80 percent, the higher the quality of the turrón.

THERE ARE TWO STYLES
Jijona (blando) in which ground almonds and honey are compressed into soft bars.

Alicante (duro), which is a crisp, hard, brittle turrón with chunks of whole almonds.

Today there are many other variations on turrón, from coconut to chocolate, all of which appear in great quantities in Spanish confectionery stores as Christmas and Three Kings Day near (as well as in The Spanish Table).

Pears Poached in Cream Sherry

Ripe autumn pears are a perfect end to the meal. Each pear makes two desserts. This recipe is even better if made in advance and left in the refrigerator to marinate for a day or two before serving.

SERVES 6

6 ripe pears, peeled, cored, and cut in half
1 bottle (750 milliliters) cream sherry
12 tablespoons Spanish orange blossom honey
1 cup whipped cream

1 Cover the pear halves with the sherry and add the honey. Bring to a boil, reduce the heat, and simmer 50 minutes, or until the pears soften. Remove the pears from the poaching liquid, then bring it to a brisk boil and reduce to ⅓ of its original volume.

2 When ready to serve, pour a large spoonful of the liquid over each pear half and top with the whipped cream.

3 Serving a chilled sweet wine like Moscatel adds another dimension of flavors as your guests relax after dinner.

Musician's Nut Tart

I am drawn to nut pastries and bought a slice of musician's tart in a bakery in Barcelona's old quarter in 1986. I have been making and enjoying them ever since.

SERVES 8

1 (10-inch) unbaked piecrust
2½ cups mixed dried fruits such as figs, dates, raisins, prunes, and/or apricots, all pitted
1½ cups sidra (apple cider or juice)
2 tablespoons butter
1 tablespoon flour
½ cup orange blossom honey
1 cup milk
½ cup PX sherry
2 egg yolks
¼ cup lemon juice (less if fruit mixture included apricots)
1½ cups mixed nuts such as negreta hazelnuts, Marcona almonds, walnuts and/or pine nuts

1 Preheat oven to 350 degrees F. Blind bake the piecrust in a 10-inch tart pan with a removable rim. To blind bake, roll out the pastry and place in the tart pan. Line the bottom and sides of the pastry with parchment paper and cover the bottom with dried beans, rice, or pastry weights. This will keep the piecrust flat and level.

2 While the empty crust is baking, place the dried fruit in a small saucepan with the sidra and bring to a boil, reduce heat, and simmer until the liquid has been absorbed. Remove from heat and let cool.

3 Melt the butter in a medium saucepan, then whisk in the flour. Add the honey, and then the milk, whisking it all together. In a separate bowl, beat the PX and egg yolks, and then whisk in to the honey mixture. Cook 15 minutes, stirring occasionally, until the mixture thickens to form a custard.

4 Purée the fruit in a food processor and add to the custard. Taste and add the lemon juice to balance the sweetness. Fill the baked pie crust with the custard mix and then the nuts, pressing them down into the mix. Bake 45 minutes.

Sources

The Spanish Table – food, wine, and tableware in the traditions of Spain and Portugal
www.spanishtable.com
Email: mailorder@spanishtable.com

The Spanish Table
1426 Western Avenue
Seattle, WA 98101
(206) 682-2827
Email: seattle@spanishtable.com

The Spanish Table
1814 San Pablo Avenue
Berkeley, CA 94702
(510) 548-1383
Email: berkeley@spanishtable.com

The Spanish Table
800 Redwood Highway
Strawberry Village 123
Mill Valley, CA 94941
(415) 388-5043
Email: millvalley@spanishtable.com

The Spanish Table
109 North Guadalupe Street
Santa Fe, NM 87501
(505) 986-0243
Email: santafe@spanishtable.com

Index

Wines and Spirits Index

Metric Conversion Chart

Liquid and Dry Measures			Temperature Conversion Chart	
U.S.	Canadian	Australian	Fahrenheit	Celsius
¼ teaspoon	1 mL	1 ml	250	120
½ teaspoon	2 mL	2 ml	275	140
1 teaspoon	5 mL	5 ml	300	150
1 tablespoon	15 mL	20 ml	325	160
¼ cup	50 mL	60 ml	350	180
⅓ cup	75 mL	80 ml	375	190
½ cup	125 mL	125 ml	400	200
⅔ cup	150 mL	170 ml	425	220
¾ cup	175 mL	190 ml	450	230
1 cup	250 mL	250 ml	475	240
1 quart	1 liter	1 litre	500	260